Praise for
The Sacrament of E

Biblical, passionate, and practical—here's a clarion call for Christians to introduce others to the God who is already present. Jerry and Stan offer a much-needed antidote to the fear many Christians feel about that dreaded word evangelism.
   Lee Strobel, author, *The Case for the Real Jesus*

Having taught evangelism around the world I have discovered that the fears are remarkably the same: What if I offend? What if I'm rejected? What if they ask me a question I can't answer? However, over time I realized that the deeper, unspoken fear was the assumption that evangelism is ultimately all about us and our skills. We suck up our courage and just hope that God will back us up! But we've got it backwards. God always goes before us because He is already there. We follow Him into the world, He doesn't follow us. Evangelism is cooperating with what God is already doing! That insight is not only liberating but it is laid out beautifully in this timely book by Root and Guthrie. They understand that evangelism means practicing God's presence as we engage in compassionate, authentic relationship with seekers and skeptics. The stories are inspiring and the discussion questions make this a perfect tool for small groups. I highly recommend it!
   Rebecca Manley Pippert
   Bestselling author, *Out of the Salt Shaker; Hope Has Its Reasons*

What a brilliant book to help us shift our paradigm of evangelism from dry obligation to a vitality of worship and a refreshing experience of God. In a world fearful to share truth Root and Guthrie give us key ingredients for evangelism that have not been fully examined for centuries. The authors have a gift for helping us understand bedrock biblical principles as well as exposing us to *tried and tested ("that is so obvious why-didn't-I-think-of-that") practical methodology. I love that the book introduces us to a wide variety of interesting people from football players, college students and restaurateurs, to Calvin, Chesterton, Moody, Rousseau, and of course C. S. Lewis. In sports ministry we say, "Always training, never playing makes athletes stale."* The Sacrament of Evangelism *will help get you into the game, revitalize your faith, and put some muscle on the dry bones of evangelism. I think I better ask my neighbor out to lunch, right now!*

Dr. Steve Connor
Director/ Facilitator
Sports Outreach International
International Sports Coalition—North America

Need confidence in sharing your faith? Let this book encourage you: you are not alone. God was there before you; He'll be there with you. Reach out boldly—this is God's deal. He is at work, and he wants you to join Him in the all-important sacrament of evangelism.

Mark Mittelberg
Author of *The Questions Christians Hope No One Will Ask* and *The Reason Why,* and coauthor (with Bill Hybels) of *Becoming a Contagious Christian*

THE 𝖘acrament OF
EVANGELISM

JERRY ROOT & STAN GUTHRIE

MOODY PUBLISHERS

CHICAGO

Library of Congress Cataloging-in-Publication Data

Root, Jerry.
The sacrament of evangelism / Jerry Root and Stan Guthrie.
    p. cm.
Includes bibliographical references.
ISBN 978-0-8024-2288-0
    1. Witness bearing (Christianity) 2. Evangelistic work. 3. Missions—Theory.
I. Guthrie, Stan. II. Title.
BV4520.R647 2011
248'.5—dc22

2010039712

Edited by Pam Pugh
Interior design: Ragont Design
Cover design: Kathryn Joachim

We hope you enjoy this book from Moody Publishers. Our goal is to provide high-quality, thought-provoking books and products that connect truth to your real needs and challenges. For more information on other books and products written and produced from a biblical perspective, go to www.moody publishers.com or write to:

Moody Publishers
820 N. LaSalle Boulevard
Chicago, IL 60610

1 3 5 7 9 10 8 6 4 2

Printed in the United States of America

DEDICATIONS

Jerry:

To my children: Jeremy, Alicia, Grady, and Jeff, who have lived the practices of this book and have seen friends come to Christ who have led others to Christ also; and to their spouses: Michelle, Zach, Leanne, and Jori that they might produce generations to reach the world for Jesus.

Stan:

To the One who has graciously allowed me to sense His presence in increasing measure amid the ups and downs of life: May I enjoy even more of Your company on the pathway while, by Your grace, introducing You to others on the way.

CONTENTS

Foreword   9

PART I: PRELIMINARIES

1. Missing Out   13
2. Getting Started   23
3. Prayer   35
4. Target Practice   47
5. The Great Commission   59

PART 2: ABIDING IN CHRIST

6. Discovering God's Love   71
7. Responding to His Love   83
8. The Spirit: God's Abiding and Empowering Presence   97
9. Character: Habits of the Heart   111
10. Mirroring the Presence of Christ in the World   123

PART 3: THE GOSPEL AND HUMANITY

11. Points of Connection   135
12. Longing: *Pilgrim*   149
13. Longing: *Lover*   161
14. Longing: *Ascetic/Saint*   173
15. Other Longings   187

PART 4: CONTENT AND FOLLOW-UP

16. Who We Are   201
17. Communication   213
18. Follow-Up #1: Jesus, Prayer, and Bible Study   227
19. Follow-Up #2: Worship, Fellowship, Obedience, and Stewardship   241
20. Reproducing Reproducers   253

Notes   263
Subject index   273
Scripture index   283
Acknowledgments   285

FOREWORD

Christians who are seriously committed to our Lord Jesus Christ's command to make disciples do not need to read one more "how-to" on the topic. But Jerry Root and Stan Guthrie have not written another one of that genre. On the contrary, they have produced a refreshing and important book.

The Sacrament of Evangelism is a prophetic call for Christians to wake up and recognize that evangelism is a sacrament, not a craft. They define *sacrament* as a place where God is present; and the sacrament of evangelism is celebrated because God is present with the witness and the person being witnessed to—and the Lord brings new life when He is met there in faith.

In Acts 16:14 we learn of a woman in Philippi named Lydia. We read that the Lord opened her heart so she could hear the good news about Jesus Christ that was spoken by the apostle Paul. The sacrament of evangelism, then, takes place when we work with God, who has prepared a harvest. It is not about us "taking Christ" to people. Rather, it is helping folks become aware of our "God who is here" now and that He wants to transform our souls and lives.

Because all people are created in God's image, they long for fellowship with Him in the way Adam and Eve experienced His presence before the fall. Because God made us to have intimacy with Him, He wants to meet us and transform us into who we were created to be.

According to Root and Guthrie, the sacrament of evangelism is practical and pastoral. It is a marriage of Great Commission (Matthew 28:18–20) and Great Commandment (Mark 12:29–31) lifestyles that should be lived wherever we are and with whomever we come to know.

This singular book is based on the Bible and sound theology. The authors illustrate their points with powerful stories from their personal experiences, and the main themes are enriched by insights from some of the best Christian minds the world has known, such as G. K. Chesterton, C. S. Lewis, George MacDonald, Dorothy L. Sayers, and Evelyn Underhill.

I intend to make *The Sacrament of Evangelism* required reading for my seminary students and recommended reading for everyone I know who desires to be a faithful disciple of the Lord Jesus Christ.

LYLE W. DORSETT
Billy Graham Professor of Evangelism
Beeson Divinity School
Samford University
Birmingham, Alabama

PART I

PRELIMINARIES

1. Missing Out
2. Getting Started
3. Prayer
4. Target Practice
5. The Great Commission

The Scriptures say the heavens declare the glory of God, but many of His works—always present with us—are missed simply because our eyes are closed.

1) MISSING OUT

We Christians are an active lot.

We serve in many areas of ministry—we staff homeless shelters, produce Christian media, build schools, send missionaries, hold prayer meetings, and sing with worship teams. Some of us, usually a minority with the "gift" of evangelism, even tell others about Jesus. If activity were the standard, we would all hear His commendation, "Well done, good and faithful servant!"[1]

But activity alone is not the standard of the Christian life—even good activity. And it never has been. In the ministry of Jesus we encounter an interesting scene:

> Now as they went on their way, Jesus entered a village. And a woman named Martha welcomed him into her house. And she had a sister called Mary, who sat at the Lord's feet and listened to his teaching. But Martha was distracted with much serving. And she went up to him and said, "Lord, do you not care that my sister has left me to serve alone? Tell her then to help me." But the Lord answered her, "Martha, Martha, you are

anxious and troubled about many things, but one thing is necessary. Mary has chosen the good portion, which will not be taken away from her."[2]

We can practice God's presence in all of life's activities, even the most menial. This includes evangelism.

We suspect that most American Christians would identify with busy, hardworking Martha, not Mary, who has simply chosen to be with Jesus. Though we theoretically know that we too ought to spend time at the feet of Jesus, in practice we feel hurried and hope that He will somehow understand. After all, "the work" has to get done, and there will be time enough to "practice His presence" later. So we resume our busy lives and ministries, and hardly ever encounter Jesus on the way.

For such people, this book will come as good news. *Really good news.* That's because, while stopping our lives to listen to Jesus can sometimes be extremely helpful, we don't have to cease all activity to hear or see God. We can experience His presence as we serve Him—especially as we do evangelism. And that presence not only will keep us going in the often hard work of evangelism, it will keep us going, period. Brother Lawrence, who washed pots for medieval monks, knew that we can practice God's presence in all of life's activities, even the most menial. This includes evangelism.

A WAY OF LOOKING AT THE WORLD

Yes, this book is about evangelism and discipleship, but on an even deeper level it is about the presence of God in the life of the believer. In fact, this volume is about the *sacrament* of evangelism. Those Christians who hold to certain kinds of sacramental theology believe that God is present in the sacraments. Whatever our doctrine about various sacraments, of course, such an approach prompts us to look for signs of God elsewhere, too.

In this book, however, we are not advocating our own position on any of the sacraments of the Christian church. We are offering a way of looking at life and the world that is open to God's presence everywhere. This approach is called *sacramental*.

Such an approach has become more accepted among evangelicals in recent years. Many Christians, particularly evangelicals, are fascinated with sacramental and liturgical approaches to faith, even if sometimes we are not too sure how biblical they are. Books on "ancient" Christianity are both common and popular.

A SACRAMENTAL APPROACH

But what does *sacrament* really mean? As the University of Notre Dame's Office of Campus Ministry states, the word "sacrament shares its roots with sacred, meaning 'filled with the presence of God.' Catholics believe that the whole world is filled with God's presence in everything from the majestic to the mundane. Whenever we respond to the gift of God's presence (sometimes also called God's grace), we call that mutual effort—God's grace and our response—sacramental."[3]

Yet there is no biblical reason that Protestants cannot also see the world sacramentally. We too believe that He is omnipresent, or everywhere present at the same time. Those who take a sacramental approach understand that God is always near and ever able to minister His grace, whether we are washing pans or telling

15

others the good news. If we do, like Jacob, we will awake from our sleep of busyness to murmur in awe, "Surely the Lord is in this place, and I did not know it."[4]

A sacramental approach to life and ministry is solidly biblical. Moses discovered it at the Red Sea with the armies of Egypt ready to attack. David found God was with him when He responded on a dusty battleground to the taunts of Goliath. Daniel found God in the den of lions. Jeremiah, abused and abandoned by men, clung to God's promise of constant companionship. And Peter, witness to the resurrection, preached with boldness on that Pentecost Sunday because he knew the Spirit of Christ was with him.

As with Peter, so with us. Evangelism is a sacrament. Those who practice it find that God is always showing up. Of course, He is already *there*, but those engaged in this sacrament begin to see Him regularly because their eyes are open to His presence. They practice His presence in their prayers for family, friends, and coworkers—even when those prayers are repeated year after year, seemingly unanswered. Hearts full of concern that others know the love and forgiveness of God keep us mindful of His nearness as we pray. Those concerned that others in their world discover the grace of Christ tend to be alert to the daily evidence of God's activity around them. They see Him when they build a relationship, when they take a risk, and when they are rejected. They also see Him when a dear friend becomes a new follower of Christ.

> It is not a question of whether God is at work in His world. It is a question of whether those who claim to follow Him will participate with Him in this sacrament.

WITH NO REGRETS

When we share the good news, we do not, to borrow a common expression, "take Christ" to anyone. Remember, He is already there. The sacrament of evangelism doesn't "do anything" to God—it does something to *us*. It opens our eyes to His work and grace. Those unaware of this sacrament, however, miss the opportunity to experience participating with this omnipotent, omnipresent God as He woos others to Himself. It is not a question of whether God is at work in His world. It is a question of whether those who claim to follow Him will participate with Him in this sacrament. This book will encourage you to discover afresh the presence of God in your world and participate in the sacrament of evangelism in ways that fit who you are.

Do you want to live sacramentally, to experience God in this way? The Westminster Catechism reminds us that we are created "to glorify God, and to enjoy him forever."[5] In our hearts we know that this glorification and enjoyment are not confined to a couple of hours a week in a church sanctuary. God has told us that He is too big for any temple. His kingdom spreads inexorably, silently, in His wake. We can—indeed, if we are true to how He made us, we *must*—glorify and enjoy Him in all of life. If we don't, we will miss out on His greatest blessings.

The sacrament of evangelism is not about getting a few more notches in our outreach belts, about following a formula. It's about working with Him, worshiping Him, and knowing Him as we participate with Him in bringing lost, sinful, and hurting people to Himself. The work will go on, with or without you. But if you choose to stand aside, God will still work, but *you* will be the loser.

How sad life would be if we never noticed the glories of the

sky. How regrettable never to notice the hues created by the setting sun: the pinks and oranges, the salmons and peach, the apri-
cot and shrimp all painted against a baby-blue canvas dancing
with color at the end of the day. How heartbreaking to have
breathed day in and day out on this marvelous planet, whose deli-
cate balances are themselves a gift, and to have missed seeing the
moon as it faithfully traces its way across the heavens. And who
could adequately describe the diamond likeness of stars twin-
kling over a desert sky on a clear autumn evening looking like gems
gleaming in the roof of an otherwise dark, cavernous universe?
Who can grasp the wonder of comets and shooting stars and
galaxies? Our lives seem charged with astonishment when we
encounter the northern lights—the black firmament coruscating
and pulsating in colors of red, blue, and green.

The Scriptures say the heavens declare the glory of God,[6] but
many of His works—always present with us—are missed simply
because our eyes are closed. Yet He is ever present and ministering grace to us. Even when His creatures rebel, He causes the sun
to rise every morning and the stars to adorn the cloudless night skies.

The Bible reminds us that the earth shows God's handiwork.
An eye rightly trained cannot help but notice the curling and
breaking of a wave onto the beach, the pause midflight of a hum-
mingbird seeming to defy gravity as it draws nectar from a petu-
nia. In fact, the petal of the flower itself—with its subtle, velvety
texture and aroma—is glorious. The laughter of a child at Christmas; the soaring of the eagle on high thermal drafts; the fresh,
falling snow that clothes the trees after their leaves have been
stripped by blustery autumn winds; here too are glories, signs
pointing to God's eternal power and divine nature.[7]

HIS WORKPLACE

There are other works of God in the world, and these too declare His glory. These are works not of creation but of *re*-creation. God is at work wooing people to Himself. Tragically, judging by our sluggish growth rates, too few churches in America are putting themselves in a place where they can see—and participate in—the work of God in the world. Yet God is too big for His purposes to be thwarted by our inactivity. He can use anyone and He certainly doesn't need us. But we will miss out on the wonder of participating with Him in His workplace.

One day a board member of a certain church invited the pastor to visit his manufacturing plant. The two men knew each other fairly well, but only in church contexts. So the pastor went, not sure what he would see. Once he got there, he saw the board member, whom he considered a solid Christian, in a whole new light. The pastor first of all was amazed at his friend's company, which he had built from scratch. He employed a sizable workforce. The design of the product reflected real genius.

During the visit, employees at the factory came up to their boss and asked complex work questions. The board member answered each one with care and insight. He knew all of his factory workers by name, often pausing to ask questions about the welfare of their children, aging parents, or how the worker's team was doing in the local bowling league. The pastor said he had no clue how kind and brilliant his friend was until he spent that day with him. Then the pastor observed: "I thought I knew my friend because I knew him at church; but I never really knew him until I got to know him in his workplace."

This book will encourage you to get to know God in *His*

workplace, to develop a sense of awe while watching firsthand as He woos people to Himself. Few activities give a sense of meaning and purpose more clearly than the privilege of leading another human being to faith in Christ and discipling that person to lead others to Christ as well.

Further, as you begin to practice the sacrament of evangelism, you will find yourself growing in spiritual maturity. What the church today finds extraordinary will become ordinary in your life—for the glory of God and your own enjoyment.

Let's get started.

Discussion Questions

I. Do you frequently or infrequently observe Christians you know sharing their faith with others? What might be the circumstances that determine the frequency you observe?

2. Do you think it is possible some do not tell others about Christ because they do not seem to experience Him in a vital way in their own daily lives? How might they experience Him more, and how might this result in sharing the gospel with greater ease?

3. Do you think that God is interested in bringing others to Himself? If He is, do you believe He might already be active in wooing others to Himself now? What might you discover about God if you were actively participating with Him in this work?

4. Why do you think so many Christians do not actively share the gospel of Christ with others who live in such proximity to them: coworkers, neighbors, friends, etc.?

5. What could you do to encourage other Christians to participate in the sacrament of evangelism so they could get to know God better in His workplace?

"If a thing is worth doing, it is worth doing badly."—*G. K. Chesterton*

2) GETTING STARTED

Every new endeavor comes with a degree of awkwardness. In fact, if you do not feel awkward in some part of your life right now, you are probably not growing. A toddler learning to walk falls down and gets bruised. A six-year-old learning to ride without training wheels crashes into the bushes. A teenager taking up skateboarding may break a wrist or sprain an ankle.

Awkwardness is a normal part of life, but it shouldn't stop us from doing what needs to be done.

Don't read this book thinking, "I will begin to share my faith when I am done." Begin *now*. It is muddled logic to believe that you will start a task once you have mastered the skill. Life doesn't work that way. No one in this world is fully skilled for what is ahead. Nobody is ever ready to get married; if we waited until we were, we would miss out on the joys and challenges of a lifelong relationship. No one is ever ready to have children; if we waited until we were, the human race would end with this generation.

It is the same thing with the sacrament of evangelism. When Jesus commissioned His disciples to go into the world and proclaim the gospel, they began awkwardly. The book of Acts is the record of the church's first attempts to make Christ known to others. The early Christians only developed some degree of competence through trial and error. They persisted in the knowledge that God called them to this great work and that He was present with them in the process.

The disciples, from the very beginning, practiced the sacrament of evangelism, and the church grew as a result.

ROOM FOR IMPROVEMENT

We commonly hear well-meaning people say, "If a job is worth doing, it is worth doing well." On the other hand, G. K. Chesterton once observed that "if a thing is worth doing, it is worth doing badly."[1] If no one is doing something that should be done, it is better that someone does it poorly than that it not be done at all.

Significant things will never be done perfectly; there is always room for improvement. This is certainly true when it comes to the sacrament of evangelism. Therefore, we are wise to get started and grow in our capacity and competence while actually doing it. Learn all you can, but don't deceive yourself into believing you will begin once you know everything, or once you have acquired perfect skill. Such a time will never come.

With that in mind, this book will encourage anyone attempting to share Christ with others, no matter how feeble you feel your efforts are. We become more proficient not simply by adding knowledge, but by applying it, because we are never more teachable than when we are in the middle of a task for which we lack skill. The insight and coaching in this book will be most valuable for the person actually engaged with the material rather than for the person for whom this subject is a mere intellectual exercise. Evangelism is a matter of the head and the heart, coupled with the practical intention to invest your life in the lives of others.

GET IN OR MISS OUT

Yet be assured that if you make a commitment to practice the sacrament of evangelism, you will grow in your knowledge of God. In Philemon 6 (NIV), the apostle Paul wrote to a friend, "I pray that you may be active in sharing your faith, so that you will have a full understanding of every good thing we have in Christ."

The result of active evangelism, he says, is "full understanding" of our relationship with the Lord. The converse seems to be (echoing chapter 1) that we will miss out on much in our Christian experience if we neglect to share Christ with others. Evangelism is not something extra for super-spiritual saints. It is for all of us, if we desire to grasp what our salvation is all about.

How might this be so? First, on a very practical level, you will be forced to field all kinds of questions about the faith. Given the complexities, interests, and histories of the people with whom we share, we will likely hear many questions that far exceed our knowledge. Few among us would attempt to write a review of a book without reading it first, for fear of appearing foolish. Neither should we ignorantly answer questions of eternal importance, not because we

> The more you share your faith, the more people will ask questions—hard questions.

might look foolish, but because the stakes are so high.

These questions must be handled with great care. We will not always know the answers, but we can learn. In the meantime, it is fine to answer a challenging query by admitting, "I am sorry that I do not know the answer; but if this is what is keeping you from faith in Christ, I will not leave a stone unturned until I can find out for you."

If we have glib answers for everything, we will lose the right to be taken seriously.

The more you share your faith, the more people will ask questions—hard questions. The more you take people and their questions seriously, the more you will grow as you dig for answers. Sharing Jesus will help you gain a fuller understanding of your life in Christ, more deeply than you are likely to gain if you are idle evangelistically. This too is evidence of the sacrament of evangelism, because in the act of wrestling with the questions of others, we discover more about God and His presence.

Second, you will grow spiritually because those with whom you share Christ will be watching to see if you are the real thing. A man said he would never put a Christian bumper sticker on his car. When asked why, he replied that he would have to start driving more responsibly.

HONEST ANSWERS

In a similar way, those who share their faith come under close scrutiny. It is not that people expect perfection from Christians—

26

they already know we aren't perfect! They do, however, want to see if we are secure enough in Christ to admit our failures and to seek forgiveness. Nonbelievers are looking for authenticity, since so often Christians are seen as hypocrites. People want to see if the Christ we preach makes a difference in our own lives. If we have glib answers for everything without respect to the complexities; and if we gloss over our failures, and the failures of the church, as if they didn't matter—we will lose the right to be taken seriously.

On the other hand, if the people scrutinizing us see that form of humility synonymous with honesty, we will gain credibility. Concurrently, we will become more mature servants of the kingdom as our lives increasingly match our message. We will discover God's presence more richly as we depend on Him and His transformative power. Those engaged in evangelism put themselves in position to gain the fuller understanding of all they have in Christ that Philemon 6 talks about.

And no matter how much we learn, we can always learn more. God is so incomprehensibly enormous and so fathomlessly deep that whatever we come to know about Him will be incomplete. Go to a bookstore and look at the rows of books. Have you read them all? Even the smartest and best educated among us can't contemplate keeping up with *human* knowledge. How in the world do we think we can grasp the reality of God? As the Lord Himself says:

For as the heavens are higher than the earth,
so are my ways higher than your ways
and my thoughts than your thoughts.[2]

We can always learn more about God—indeed, if we are wise, we *must* learn more. But whether you know a little or a lot, if you practice the sacrament of evangelism, you will experience the presence of God in your life—and in the lives of others.

FRESHMAN FOOTBALL

Here's how it started out for Jerry. He became a Christian his freshman year at Whittier College in California. The people who faithfully shared Christ with him were eager to tell others in their world about Jesus' love and forgiveness. Grateful they shared with him, Jerry caught their enthusiasm for evangelism.

Jerry, who majored in physical education at Whittier, was a freshman football player who looked up to one of the senior captains on the varsity team. This young man's name was Dave, and he did not have a relationship with Christ. Dave was a preseason All-American, and he was a leader whom Jerry greatly admired.

The rules back then required freshmen to play one year of freshman ball before they could move up to the varsity roster. During that season, Jerry chose to wear number 50 because it was Dave's varsity number. Dave, as expected, had an outstanding year. During the last varsity game of the season, the freshmen were allowed to suit up and stand on the sidelines (even though they weren't allowed to play). As Jerry walked up to the field with Dave that night, Jerry tried to engage his hero in small talk.

"You know, Dave," Jerry said, "everyone's saying you will probably be selected as an All-American after the season is over."

"Yeah, that's what they tell me," Dave replied in his gravelly voice. "But you know what would mean even more to me than that?"

"What's that?"

"It would even mean more to me to come back next year and see you wearing my jersey number."

Talk about inspiring! Jerry began to wonder whether God might want him to share Christ with Dave. When the season was over, he began dropping by to see Dave each week and invite him to come to a Christian group that met Sunday evenings at a large house just off campus. Dave would always give the same answer: "No, Jerry, I can't go this week; but come by next week and check in with me." This went on week after week.

Jerry began praying earnestly to the God he was only beginning to come to know himself. Finally, to Jerry's surprise, the day came when Dave answered, "You know, I could probably use something like that right now in my life."

That Sunday night, the house was packed, and excitement was in the air. The speaker was Dick Day, a gifted evangelist. Jerry had heard him many times before and was pleased that Dave would get to hear the gospel from one of the best. And Jerry was not disappointed.

A porch load of onlookers watched as the All-American football star invited Christ, who was already there, into his life.

After the presentation, Dick went outside and leaned against the railing that outlined the big wraparound front porch. Jerry introduced the two of them, Dick facing the house and Dave facing Dick. Dave had some questions, and after a few moments the two of them were talking about the love of Christ and the power and meaning of His death and resurrection. As the conversation went on, Dave was unaware of the large crowed that was gathering behind him. Everyone knew who he was and waited breathlessly as the two men discussed the gospel.

"You know, Dave, God loves every one of us," Dick said. With a twinkle in his eye, he added, "He loves all of these people on the porch behind you, too!" Intent on hearing about Jesus, Dave hadn't been aware of the crowd. Turning and looking at the gathering, Dave cracked, "Well, Dick, God's not very picky, is He?" Jerry and the others there howled with laughter.

As the conversation progressed, Dave became serious once again and asked Dick, "What do I have to do to become a Christian?" Dick replied, "Just ask Jesus into your life."

So Dave simply looked up into the sky and said, "Jesus, come in!" A porch load of onlookers watched as the All-American football star invited Christ, who was already there, into his life. Dave was unashamed and eager to know the God who loved him so much.

At the time Jerry thought how remarkable it is that God uses any of us to work with Him in calling people to trust in Him. Jerry didn't know all that much and at times felt awkward, but he was privileged to see God in His workplace, bringing another sinner to Himself. Evangelism is a prime means of practicing the Lord's presence and watching Him faithfully exhibit His nearness and grace.

NOT ALL HAPPY ENDINGS, BUT . . .

Not every story will turn out exactly as this one did, however. Awkwardness may be the least of your problems. It may be that those with whom you share the good news will turn against you;

they may even make life more difficult for you. Stan, like many other ordinary Christians trying to share the good news, has seen friends, acquaintances, and strangers mock his beliefs. While derisive laughter, uncomfortable silence, or the loss of a friendship never killed anyone, they are nevertheless painful events in the life of the Christian willing to do the work of evangelism.

The warnings about this kind of response and worse are both numerous and stark in the Bible.

Then they will deliver you up to tribulation and put you to death, and you will be hated by all nations for my name's sake.[3]

Indeed, all who desire to live a godly life in Christ Jesus will be persecuted.[4]

The apostle Paul himself faced numerous assassination attempts for his bold proclamation of the gospel. He was flogged and beaten. To the Jewish leaders living in Rome, a captive Paul stated, "It is because of the hope of Israel that I am wearing this chain."[5] Of course, before he came to know the risen Lord, Paul himself had gleefully persecuted Christians.

Sometimes you may seem to whiff spiritually, not understanding how your efforts fit into the grand scheme of God's purposes and plans.

You too may endure hostility from contemporary Pauls. Perhaps this is one of the things the apostle is implying in Colossians 1:24: "Now I rejoice in my sufferings for your sake, and in my flesh I am filling up what is lacking in Christ's afflictions for the sake of his body, that is, the church." Christ suffered that we might know Him, and He may allow us the privilege of suffering while others come to know Him. Such suffering, however, will certainly draw you closer to God as you seek His comfort and guidance.

At times as you practice this sacrament, you may think that you have struck out. But if you are afraid of striking out, don't play baseball. Of course, if you don't, you will never know the joy of hitting a home run. It is the same with telling others about Jesus. Sometimes you may seem to whiff spiritually, not understanding how your efforts fit into the grand scheme of God's purposes and plans. There will be other times when you feel like you just hit a home run. You will enter into the joy of someone who has just understood the love and forgiveness of God.

The more you patiently share the gospel with others, the more likely you are to see a wide range of responses. Some people may hear it for the first time and express incredulity and perhaps contempt. Others may get a nudge toward Christ, especially if you are part of a long line of people God has been sending to them. But you may never know the result of your efforts until heaven.

The results belong to Him, but His presence, in a sense, will belong to you. But you have to get started.

Discussion Questions

I. What about evangelism makes you feel awkward? Do you believe practice might diminish the awkwardness? Why? Or, why not?

2. Do you think sharing Christ with others would help you to develop a more robust understanding of your own faith in Christ? Do you think if others heard you speak of Jesus to them, it might affect the way you act toward them? How might this be so?

3. If you saw other Christians loving people enough to share the gospel more frequently, would their example influence you to share more? Why? Or, why not?

4. What could you do to influence others to share the gospel more?

5. Not everyone with whom you share the gospel will respond positively. Have you had instances when this was so? What happened? Have you had other instances where others did draw closer to Christ? What happened? Would you agree that the joy of seeing people respond to Christ is worth the occasional times of rejection?

We can move forward confidently into the harvest field, knowing that God is already present.

3) PRAYER

Getting started in evangelism can seem extremely daunting, especially if you are an introvert or are worried about how others might perceive you. What if people laugh at or reject me? What if I become tongue-tied or confused? What if I offend someone?

Stan recently attempted to share the gospel with his physical therapist, a Hindu from India, and was stymied by this gentle man's lack of interest in any faith that claimed to be the only way. The conversation seemingly went nowhere, and Stan was relieved after a few minutes of earnest evangelism to return to the more comfortable territory of his physical recovery after surgery. Many of us who are otherwise fearless tremble, like a kindergartner facing her first day of school, over speaking with someone about Jesus.

We could use the usual words to buck up your courage for the evangelistic challenge:

- people aren't usually as hostile to the gospel as we fear (though sometimes they are)

- we don't have to be able to answer every intellectual question to gain someone's interest
- evangelism can be fun
- do your best and leave the results in God's hands

These prescriptions, and many more, may all be true enough, but they provide little defense against the stage fright and knocking knees that so often accompany our first feeble attempts to share Christ with our friends, neighbors, and coworkers. The spirit indeed may be willing, but the flesh can be frustratingly weak. How much easier it would be to begin evangelizing if we didn't have to face the other person! What if we could start the sacrament of evangelism in the privacy of our homes?

THE GROUNDWORK

The truth is, we can, and in fact this is probably the best way. This book aims to help us see life in general and evangelism in particular *sacramentally*—recognizing that God is already present. The sacramental evangelist needs to grasp the double-edged fact that not only is the Creator of the universe with *us* in our halting efforts to spread His good news, but He is also already with the *other person* whom we want to bless. And if God is already with us and our friend, doesn't it make perfect sense to tap into His continuing presence and power through prayer?

That's why we believe the best way to begin sacramental evangelism is with prayer. Every Christian, no matter if knowledgeable or a novice, no matter if persecuted or popular, can pray to the listening God who is already *here*. Prayer and practicing

God's presence are not some fancy add-ons to our sacramental evangelism. They are its engine.

Think of the story of Philip and the Ethiopian eunuch.[1] An active evangelist,[2] Philip was sent by a heavenly messenger southwards, where he met an Ethiopian court official on the road to Gaza. The Spirit, already present there, told Philip to go alongside the official, who was reading Isaiah. Philip did so, eventually telling his new friend "the good news about Jesus." Listening and praying to God, Philip was practicing sacramental evangelism, blessing an ancient nation with a Christian presence that continues to this day.

One way to pray to the God who is already present with us and who is also with the person we wish to reach is to ask that the other person's heart be opened to the gospel. The Lord, in a sense, stands both between us and above us. There is more involved in sacramental evangelism than horizontal, one-on-one witnessing. Before you do that necessary act, be sure to start your vertical ministry: pray. Then God, who loves this person more than you do anyway, will begin to do His work from above, down into the heart of the person, before you even open your mouth. You may even find that God was already working before you offered any prayers.

PLANT SEEDS AND FLAGS

But whether such prayers are a request for God's grace or a response to it, we cannot neglect them. God uses those prayers to bring people to Himself in a variety of ways. Jerry once had a pastor who would ask the congregation, "If God answered every prayer you prayed this last week, would there be anybody new in Christ's kingdom?" If we want to see people come to Christ, sacramental evangelists must be praying evangelists.

God wants us to make Him known in the places we frequent each day: our neighborhoods, our workplaces, our schools.

If we are not praying for people in our spheres of influence, we are probably missing a host of opportunities to share Christ. Jesus made it clear that many, many people want to hear about His love and forgiveness. The problem, Jesus claimed, was not with uninterested hearers but with too few followers willing to speak up.

> And Jesus went throughout all the cities and villages, teaching in their synagogues and proclaiming the gospel of the kingdom and healing every disease and every affliction. When he saw the crowds, he had compassion for them, because they were harassed and helpless, like sheep without a shepherd. Then he said to his disciples, "The harvest is plentiful, but the laborers are few; therefore pray earnestly to the Lord of the harvest to send out laborers into his harvest."[3]

Jesus said that people want to hear about God and His love for them, but few of His followers are prepared to help them do so. The first prayer of the sacramental evangelist, then, is for laborers. And as we pray for laborers, we will naturally pray for those waiting to hear.

Then as we begin to faithfully pray for those around us to come to faith, we are more likely to pick up on the clues in our conversations with them indicating their spiritual thirst. This knowledge will enable us to follow the conversation where God leads. Begin your awkward first steps in evangelism by praying regularly for friends and acquaintances in your world who do not yet know Christ. When you do, you will see God at work.

Related to this, Christians ought to plant God's flag wherever they are called, using the unique opportunities and relationships He provides. As the apostle Paul said, God determined our allotted times and boundary places that we should seek Him.[4] Besides our expected commitment to global missions, God wants us to make Him known in the places we frequent each day: our neighborhoods, our workplaces, our schools, and so forth. We can't plant His flag everywhere, but we can plant it where we live. Because you already live in the time and place of God's world determined by Him, you can legitimately see your life as a unique call to be His ambassador to that place.[5]

IT STARTED WITH LUNCH

The following true story will encourage you to get started. It may also help you to see that sacramental evangelism that begins with prayer is a nonthreatening and fairly easy way to connect with people you already care about but with whom you have been hesitant to speak openly and frankly about Christ.

Years ago, Jerry chose to eat lunch four workdays a week at a local restaurant, where he could plant his flag and get some work done before continuing with the rest of his day. The owner of the restaurant was named Brad. Jerry put him on his daily prayer list, asking that Brad, would come to faith in Christ.

Every day when Jerry saw Brad, he made a point to greet him

and, circumstances permitting, to engage in a little small talk. Jerry would ask how business was going. He would compliment Brad for some item on the menu he particularly enjoyed. Other times Jerry would introduce the owner to whomever he brought to the restaurant that day. Brad was pleased that Jerry was introducing so many new customers to his restaurant. Jerry even took his family to eat there one evening.

> **Jerry assured Brad that he was indeed praying for him and never missed a day. Then, to Jerry's surprise, Brad asked if he would pray for his boys.**

After about three weeks of this, Jerry took the next step. "You know, Brad," he said to him, "I pray for you every day. I never miss." That was all. Now Jerry has said this often enough to various people and has never encountered someone who took offense. Jerry has never been asked to stop this kind of praying. While we're not saying that there will never be someone one day who might tell us to stop it, Jerry's experience is that most people are grateful for prayers on their behalf.

Brad, however, *was* a bit taken back by Jerry's announcement, so next to nothing more was said about it. Jerry and Brad returned to their small talk, and so it went each day for the next few weeks. That was as aggressive as Jerry became in his evangelistic efforts.

About three weeks passed before Jerry again mentioned to Brad that he was praying for him. Brad stopped and looked him right in the eye. "You mentioned that a few weeks ago," Brad answered, "and I didn't really think you were doing it. But if you are saying it again today, you must really be praying for me." Jerry assured Brad that he was indeed praying for him and never missed a day. Then, to Jerry's surprise, Brad asked if he would pray for his boys, but he didn't elaborate. Jerry wrote their names down and included them in his daily prayers.

That evening at dinner Jerry mentioned to his family that Brad had requested prayer for his boys. "Dad, I know one of his sons," said Jerry's daughter Alicia. "He goes to my school." Five months later, Alicia came running home from youth group. One of the boys at her school had invited Brad's son to the youth group, and that evening he had given his heart to Jesus. Jerry's children not only *believe* that God answers these kinds of prayers, they *know* it. They have *seen* the sacrament of evangelism, discovering the active presence of God in their world.

The weeks went by as Jerry continued practicing the sacrament. He would engage in small talk with Brad four times a week. About every third week, he would remind him of his daily prayers for him and his boys. Anyone can do this; *anyone.* One day, as Jerry was enjoying a working lunch, Brad approached the table. "Jerry," he said, "can I talk with you after lunch today?"

"Sure," Jerry said, and arranged to clear his schedule for the afternoon. The two men walked down the street to a coffee shop. There the usually reserved Brad poured out his heart, describing some sorrowful problems in his life. Brad wanted a listening ear and some advice. In the many months Jerry had known him as an acquaintance, they had never engaged in a conversation of this depth. But Brad opened up to him so freely because he knew that Jerry cared for him. For all that Jerry knew, he might have been the only person in Brad's immediate world with whom he felt free to share such things.

After hearing Brad's story over the next two hours, Jerry

finally said, "I think you need Jesus in your life." Then, in the next five minutes, he shared the gospel simply and directly. Brad, to Jerry's surprise, agreed that he needed Jesus. But Brad said he didn't want to give Christ his life as it was. He wanted to work on some things first, and then, when his life was in top shape, he would offer it to Christ.

Brad apparently had never heard the old hymn "Just as I Am," and Jerry didn't force his friend to first dot his theological i's and cross his theological t's. When you are practicing the sacrament of evangelism, there is no need to press. God is present.

So instead, Jerry replied, "You go on ahead and do what you think is best; but if you find that your way is not working, give me a call." Jerry continued to visit the restaurant, engaging in small talk as before. And every third week he reminded Brad of his daily prayers.

About five months later, Brad came to Jerry's office to tell him that his way wasn't working and that he was ready to give his heart to Jesus. God had been present and working in Brad's life all along, as Jerry knew. After that, Jerry and Brad started meeting regularly to discover how one might grow in a new relationship with Christ.

This story shows that anyone can begin to share Christ. You don't have to be pushy. You don't have to know it all. You don't need the latest surefire evangelistic technique. All you have to do is start praying for others in your world and occasionally tell them about those prayers. We cannot guarantee that you will always see the same results. The results, after all, are ultimately in God's hands. But you can move forward confidently into the harvest field, knowing that God is already present.

We believe that if you do, many of your relationships will go in directions that can only be attributed to the Lord of the harvest. This approach will not work the same way with every person, because we are all different, and the Spirit works as He wills to bring new life. But it is a quietly powerful way for anyone to start practicing the sacrament of evangelism—even you.

Discussion Questions

I. Who are the people in your world (or sphere of influence) you could start praying for? What is preventing you from praying for them?

2. Have you ever prayed daily for another person to come to Christ and told that person? What happened? If you haven't prayed daily for someone and told them that you did, why not begin now? Can you imagine the encouragement this person might feel?

3. Jesus asked His followers to pray for God to raise up laborers to go out into their worlds and harvest souls for His kingdom. He said the fields were ready for harvest; in other words, there are more people who want to know than who are willing to tell. What prevents you from praying for more people to be willing to share the gospel? What do you think might happen to you if you prayed regularly for God to motivate more people to share the gospel?

4. Where could you intentionally plant Christ's flag and share the gospel as opportunity allows? Is it possible that God might strategically have put you in your sphere of influence? What might happen if you assumed responsibility for this place? Could you discover more of God in this place?

5. What would happen to your faith if you started seeing others in your world coming to faith in Christ? What would happen in your church if this occurred with greater frequency among regular attendees? What could happen in our world?

If we do not understand our target, the heart of the audience, the message will most likely become irrelevant.

4) TARGET PRACTICE

Jerry sometimes places a bullet into the hands of his students and asks them to describe it. The descriptions soon follow: The object is cylindrical in shape, flat on one end and rounded and domelike on the other; the domed end is made of lead, the flat end of brass; it is about an inch and a half long and a third of an inch wide. Further, writing on the flat end reads, "Winchester .38 Special." Careful observation yields more details than you might expect.

This attempt at description is something like what an exegete does when poring over a text of Scripture.

A good exegete—someone who digs into the message of Scripture in order to grasp the details of its words, grammar, and cultural context—reminds us that as much as we think we know the Bible, there are always further depths to explore. But while the text is objective fact, interpretations of the text are subjective. As literary and cultural critic Terry Eagleton observed, "The subjective is a matter of value, while the world is a matter of fact."[1]

Of course it is best when what we value is consistent with what is fact. The apostle Paul captured the need for congruence between facts and values when he asserted that belief in the resurrection (a value) must correspond with an actual resurrection (a fact):

> And if Christ has not been raised, your faith is futile and you are still in your sins. Then those also who have fallen asleep in Christ have perished. If in Christ we have hope in this life only, we are of all people most to be pitied.[2]

Nevertheless, facts are complex. Even those facts we think we understand well should be accompanied by the humility of knowing there is always more to learn. Even a truth understood can be plumbed more deeply. We can apply that truth to questions we have yet to ask, and we can understand it in relation to other truths. In other words, genuine understanding tends to be integrated and allows us to move toward a more holistic grasp of reality.

For the Christian seeker of truth, this holistic understanding is consistent with a sacramental grasp of reality that is infused with the very presence of God. Our proclamation of biblical truth generally and the gospel specifically becomes deeper and more nuanced because of our respect for the complexity and richness of the message we share and for the God who is near.

KNOW YOUR AUDIENCE

Knowing a biblical text, like knowing the gospel, is a lot like describing a bullet. But such knowledge does not guarantee you can present the gospel effectively any more than describing a bullet well guarantees you can hit a target with it. We need more.

Evangelists must also know their audiences. We need to become acquainted with the people around us in order to communicate clearly with them. As we have been saying, this world where people live is invaded with the very presence of God. To discover God's work in the world is to engage in a sacramental activity.

While it is important to know the gospel message, it is equally important to know the audience. To continue the metaphor, let's call these people the target. (This means that we need to reach them in love, not shoot at them.) If the gospel—the bullet—is to gain a hearing, people—the target—need to understand the vitality of its message in relationship to their fears, their relational struggles, and their personal failures. In essence, how does the living Christ, showing up in the message, help people deal with their sins and the host of consequences that result from those sins?

If we do not understand our target, the heart of the audience, the message will most likely become irrelevant. Ralph Waldo Emerson addressed the Divinity School at Harvard College in 1838 and made this same point:

> I once heard a preacher who sorely tempted me to say I would go to church no more. . . . A snowstorm was falling around us. The snowstorm was real, the preacher merely spectral, and the eye felt the sad contrast in looking at him, and then out of the window behind him into the beautiful meteor of the snow. He had lived in vain. He had no one word intimating that he had laughed or wept, was married or in love, had been commended, or cheated, or chagrined. If he had ever lived and acted, we were none the wiser for it. The capital secret of his profession, namely, to convert life into truth, he had not

learned. Not one fact in all his experience had he yet imported into his doctrine. This man had ploughed and planted and talked and bought and sold; he had read books; he had eaten and drunken; his head aches, his heart throbs; he smiles and suffers; yet was there not a surmise, a hint, in all the discourse, that he had ever lived at all. Not a line did he draw out of real history.[3]

The preacher whom Emerson heard that day failed to connect the gospel to the real world, where his audience lived each day. Consequently, he missed his target. It is safe to say that the greatest principle of Christian proclamation is: *The Word became flesh and dwelt among us.*[4] The gospel hits the mark when it is couched in empathy for those who hear it. Jesus looked out on His audiences with compassion (Matthew 9:36). So the question of the hour is: How can the person proclaiming the gospel grow in compassion and empathy? Certainly these character qualities assume that we know ourselves.

> "Without knowledge of God there can be no knowledge of self."

KNOW YOURSELF

The analogy of bullets and targets thus requires one other element to be complete. We must also consider the gun, which is the life of the person who delivers the message (the bullet) to the audience (the target). Again, this is an analogy. We are not advocating violence or coercion with the metaphor of a gun. We are saying that sacramental evangelists need to be aware—both aware of themselves as well as aware of God's presence and purpose in their lives.

"Without knowledge of self there is no knowledge of God," Calvin says at the beginning of his *Institutes of the Christian Religion*. "Nearly all the wisdom we possess, that is to say, true and sound wisdom, consists of two parts: the knowledge of God and of ourselves. . . . The knowledge of ourselves not only arouses us to seek God, but also, as it were, leads us by the hand to find him."

Later, Calvin adds, "Without knowledge of God there can be no knowledge of self. Again, it is certain that man never achieves a clear knowledge of himself unless he has first looked upon God's face, and then descends from contemplating him to scrutinize himself."[5]

There is much we do not know about ourselves apart from God—and much we can discover only in communion with Him. The good news is that He loves us, and His love is not conditioned on our behavior. It is not increased by our performance nor diminished by our failures. We can come to Him freely because His love was freely given when we were wayward and unresponsive. The Scriptures say, "But God shows his love for us in that while we were still sinners, Christ died for us" (Romans 5:8). Further, if His love is not diminished by our shortcomings and sin, then we can look honestly at our failures in the light of His steady presence. We need not hide behind a veneer of rationalization and pretense. We can safely own the truth about ourselves.

The real presence of Christ in our lives makes it possible to look openly and honestly at ourselves. This looking allows the evangelist to deliver the gospel with honesty. When we do this without fear, we authenticate the sacrament of evangelism. It shows that we understand the message beyond the bare words and grammar. It reveals that we understand the gospel in our own lives and desperately cling to God's grace and love. In fact, empathy for your audience will begin to emerge because you start to see others with the same sort of compassion with which Christ has loved you.

But we must be careful not to allow ourselves to fall into too much navel-gazing. With humility, we (the gun) must practice the sacrament of evangelism by sharing the message (the bullet) with other imperfect people (the target). We should not wait while we attempt to figure everything out. We should start right away. Let's examine why a little more closely in the balance of this chapter.

KNOW YOUR METHOD

In Shakespeare's *Hamlet*, Polonius, the chief counsel of King Claudius, is sent to spy on the antic Prince of Denmark, who is spouting absurdities. After speaking with the ostensibly crazy man for some time, finally Polonius turns to the audience. "Though this be madness," he says, "yet there is method in't."[6]

It may seem crazy to suggest toward the *beginning* of a book on evangelism that you start doing the work of an evangelist right away. You might expect that it is best to wait until you have the knowledge and skills to share your faith. After all, evangelism can be touch and go. People's eternal destinies hang in the balance; you want to get it right. You wouldn't think of jumping out of an airplane and risking your physical life without knowing all the basics of skydiving. Why should evangelism—where the stakes are even higher—be any different?

But there is a method, as Polonius might say, to our madness. As we have indicated already, attempting to do evangelism when you know you don't have all the answers will make you more teachable. But we have other reasons. If you really believe that evangelism is a sacrament—that God is already present with you and with the person you seek to reach, and that you can expect to see God showing up when you step out in faith—then you need not fear. As King David exulted:

> **G**od's nearness, His immanence, encourages us to take risks, knowing that He is present to support us.

> For you are my lamp, O Lord,
> and my God lightens my darkness.
> For by you I can run against a troop,
> and by my God I can leap over a wall.
> This God—his way is perfect;
> the word of the Lord proves true;
> he is a shield for all those who take refuge in him.
> For who is God, but the Lord?
> And who is a rock, except our God?
> This God is my strong refuge
> and has made my way blameless.
> He made my feet like the feet of a deer
> and set me secure on the heights.
> He trains my hands for war,
> so that my arms can bend a bow of bronze.

You have given me the shield of your salvation,
and your gentleness made me great.[7]

God's nearness, His immanence, encourages us to take risks, knowing that He is present to support us. It is not all up to us, thank God. We are to do our best and leave the results to Him. As the great missionary pioneer William Carey said, "Expect great things; attempt great things."[8] If you never take a risk for God, you will never see Him intervene in powerful and unmistakable ways. As the Scripture says, "For the eyes of the Lord move to and fro throughout the earth that He may strongly support those whose heart is completely His."[9] Are you putting yourself in the kinds of situations that require God to show Himself? Put God first, and He will not disappoint you.

BUILD A CULTURE OF EVANGELISM

There is another reason you should get started now. Statistics about Western churches and evangelism are pretty dismal. Whether due to a lack of commitment or know-how, we are making very little progress in winning people to Christ.[10] While there are many faithful saints in our churches, and you may be able to find a few people who share your passion to see God at work in evangelism, this will probably be the exception rather than the rule. While this is a tragic situation, it is neither without biblical precedent nor without biblical hope.

In the book of Judges, we encounter a verse, repeated twice in the book, which reads, "In those days there was no king in Israel. Everyone did what was right in his own eyes."[11] Some expositors and scholars have suggested that this statement of Israel's social and moral declension is key for making sense of Judges—and not without reason. The appalling events that unfold in the unvarnished narrative surely indicate that the nation suffered politically and spiritually because it lacked godly leadership.

However, the key verse comes earlier. Judges 2:10b reads, "And there arose another generation after them who did not know the Lord or the work he had done for Israel." It is an indicting statement. The generation of which it speaks followed those who had finally conquered the Promised Land with Joshua.

They were the children of those who had tasted manna in the wilderness each day and had witnessed the glory of God as He appeared daily as a cloud above the tabernacle and at night as a pillar of fire. Their parents had witnessed the parting of the waters of the Jordan as they crossed the riverbed on dry land. They were the children of those who watched in reverent awe as the mighty power of God caused the great walls of Jericho to come crashing down.

How is it that these parents, who had seen and done so much, had neglected to tell their children about the plan and purposes of God? They had walked with God. They had experienced His goodness and glory. How could they *not* pass this knowledge on? The text does not say, but we see the tragic results all too clearly.

How could the new generation possibly recover and grow in the ways of God without seasoned instructors, when its members had never "done it" themselves? This is the challenge of the sacramental evangelist, who today likely has precious few role models willing to show him or her the spiritual ropes. To overcome this glaring kind of handicap, the new generation in the book of Judges would have to learn by trial and error. It would have to take steps of faith, receive its lumps, and wait for God's deliverance.

And we see many examples in Judges of flawed and sinful

people—such as Barak and Gideon—who learned both to expect great things and attempt great things. Then these heroes needed to pass on the things they learned about God's presence and power to succeeding generations. Unfortunately, the book is a sad chronicle of repeated cycles of oppression, repentance, deliverance, and decline. God's people in Israel's Dark Ages were never able to quite pass their spiritual lessons and experience on to their children.

That seems to be the problem with evangelism today. You can always find faithful stalwarts willing to step out in faith to share the good news. (Because you are reading this book, you may be one of them.) The problem is that while some churches have figured out how to make outreach among their members a significant part of their culture, most have not. Evangelism has become the hobby of the few, rather than a joyful expectation of all. Thus, those who wish to obey this high calling often have to start from scratch.

Someone has to get started, and *you* can be that person. If evangelism is a vital but neglected calling of the church in the world, we must learn how to do it ourselves. Then, as we figure out what we are doing, we can build a culture of evangelism and pass on what we have learned. When we do this, future generations will also experience God moving through them to bless their neighbors and the world.

This is why we say this book will be most valuable for people who are eager to get started now. There is no substitute for actually *doing* it. This book's words are for those seeking encouragement *along the way*, rather than for those who see evangelism as a historical curiosity or as someone else's responsibility.

This is the method to our madness.

Discussion Questions

1. If, like the bullet, the gospel is something that can be described, how would you describe it? What are the essential elements, the bare bones that one needs to know to come to faith in Christ?

2. What is it about others would you be wise to know in order to connect the gospel to them in their world? How could you hit the mark with your message?

3. What is it about yourself would you be wise to understand in order to share the gospel honestly and without pretense? How does this self-knowledge give you greater credibility when telling others about Christ?

4. In what ways can you expect God to reveal Himself in the message (the bullet)? How might He reveal Himself in the response of the hearers (the target)? How might He reveal Himself in your own life (the gun) as a messenger of His grace? Can you begin to see something of the presence of God in every facet of evangelism?

5. Will the generation that follows yours know God? If not, what will your generation have failed to do? What can you do now in your sphere of influence so that the next generation knows and loves God?

*Must we dichotomize social
and proclamational ministry?
Too many of us possess an either/or
approach to the Great Commission.*

5) THE GREAT COMMISSION

Before we go farther along the path of sacramental evangelism, we cannot avoid a brief stop to consider the Great Commission—the challenge Jesus gave to His disciples (and, by extension, to us) before He ascended into heaven. Here is how Matthew describes it:

> And Jesus came and said to them, "All authority in heaven and on earth has been given to me. Go therefore and make disciples of all nations, baptizing them in the name of the Father and of the Son and of the Holy Spirit, teaching them to observe all that I have commanded you. And behold, I am with you always, to the end of the age."[1]

Luke, the physician who traveled with Paul and who gave us the gospel that bears his name as well as the book of Acts, in that gospel quotes Jesus saying:

Thus it is written, that the Christ should suffer and on the third day rise from the dead, and that repentance and forgiveness of sins should be proclaimed in his name to all nations, beginning from Jerusalem. You are witnesses of these things. And behold, I am sending the promise of my Father upon you.[2]

In Acts, the sequel to Luke, the physician provides this scene just before the ascension:

So when they had come together, they asked him, "Lord, will you at this time restore the kingdom to Israel?" He said to them, "It is not for you to know times or seasons that the Father has fixed by his own authority. But you will receive power when the Holy Spirit has come upon you, and you will be my witnesses in Jerusalem and in all Judea and Samaria, and to the end of the earth."[3]

The Great Commission, however it is worded in the New Testament, refers ultimately to the challenge Jesus set before His followers to go and make disciples in the power of the Spirit and in the knowledge that He would sacramentally be with them.

The command is unambiguous, so our first task is to decide whether or not to obey. Some in the missions movement have suggested that if we decide not to, God's work in the world somehow will not get done. This is kind of like saying that if a professor passes out an exam and you refuse to take it, the exam will not take place. No, the exam still comes, but *you* miss out. In the same way God's work in the world does not suffer when His people do not do what they ought—*they* do.

God's power is not conditioned by our performance. His ultimate will is never in jeopardy. What is at risk is our opportunity to be a part of what He is doing. If we fail to participate, the blessing of His presence and power will alight elsewhere. As Mordecai warned Esther, "For if you keep silent at this time, relief and deliverance will rise for the Jews from another place, but you and your father's house will perish. And who knows whether you have not come to the kingdom for such a time as this?"[4]

IN THE THICK OF THINGS

A head football coach always has a game plan. If a player fails to do what the coach directs, the game plan is not at risk. It is the athlete's opportunity to participate that is in question. The athlete can either get in the game or sit on the bench, allowing others to take his place. The choice is ours. Don't you want to be in the thick of things, rather than watching from the sideline? When we obey the Great Commission, we are privileged to participate in God's game plan. Like a great coach, the Lord knows our strengths and weaknesses and puts us in situations where we can succeed. More than that, unlike any coach, God steps onto the field with us. And seldom are we more aware of His presence than when we get into the game.

> In the very act of putting our foot over the side of the boat, we sense that Christ is present.

George MacDonald once wrote, "Obedience is the opener of

eyes."[5] He meant that the reason for an act of obedience becomes clearer the more one obeys. As Jesus said, "But whoever does what is true comes to the light, so that it may be clearly seen that his works have been carried out in God."[6]

The flip side is also true. Disobedience, followed by rationalizations and justifications of that disobedience, makes one morally blind. Paul wrote that we "suppress the truth by [our] wickedness."[7]

The sacramental presence of Christ is manifest in each act of obedience. That is because it is by His grace alone that we can obey in the first place. Thus, if we are obeying, we can be sure God is already working. As Dietrich Bonhoeffer said, "Only he who believes is obedient, and only he who is obedient believes."[8]

A case in point is Peter's brief walk on the water.[9] While Peter ultimately failed because he took his eyes off Jesus, we must not forget that he was the only one to get out of the boat. When the apostles saw Christ walking toward them, Peter cried out, "Lord, if it's you, tell me to come to you on the water." Jesus simply said, "Come."

This was an imperative. Peter could have written books about how he might have walked on the water, and they might have made for interesting reading. But Peter would never have felt the presence of Christ and His sustaining power on the water if he had not put his foot over the gunnels of the boat. In those moments of obedience, Peter was sustained and the grace of God came to him.

So it is with the sacrament of evangelism. In the very act of putting our foot over the side of the boat, we sense that Christ is present. Fear gives way to peace, then excitement, as we see Him use our feeble, faltering gifts for His glory. Working alongside God, Paul knew the joy of such sacramental, and sacrificial, evangelism:

Working together with him, then, we appeal to you not to receive the grace of God in vain. . . .

Behold, now is the favorable time; behold, now is the day of salvation. We put no obstacle in anyone's way, so that no fault may be found with our ministry, but as servants of God we commend ourselves in every way: by great endurance, in afflictions, hardships, calamities, beatings, imprisonments, riots, labors, sleepless nights, hunger; by purity, knowledge, patience, kindness, the Holy Spirit, genuine love; by truthful speech, and the power of God; with the weapons of righteousness for the right hand and for the left; through honor and dishonor, through slander and praise. We are treated as impostors, and yet are true; as unknown, and yet well known; as dying, and behold, we live; as punished, and yet not killed; as sorrowful, yet always rejoicing; as poor, yet making many rich; as having nothing, yet possessing everything.[10]

> **W**e can't help but wonder how many injustices are perpetrated because Christ is not ruling in the hearts of people who remain outside His kingdom.

In this kind of obedience we lose nothing and gain everything. We can be confident that the Lord is at work sustaining us and leading the way in every evangelistic encounter, no matter the hardships. Let us reflect on Jim Elliot's famous dictum: "He is no fool who gives what he cannot keep to gain what he cannot lose."[11]

WHAT EXACTLY DID HE MEAN?

Yet we must probe the nature of that evangelism a little bit more before moving on. Making disciples by proclaiming the good news seems fairly straightforward. Nevertheless, many of us are not very fruitful and sometimes seem relatively unconcerned about it.

Of course, as clear as the command to spread the gospel of the kingdom appears to be two millennia later, debates about what Jesus really meant continue to roil the church. Sometimes it seems as if the less actual work is done in response to the Great Commission, the more interesting the rhetoric becomes. We flawed and fallen creatures will justify whatever we are doing, or not doing, saying that Jesus told us so.

The dialogue is alive and well in the evangelical church. Some say that God really wants us, like Christ, to simply demonstrate the kingdom. This, advocates say, consists in alleviating the burdens of the poor, addressing matters of social inequality, protecting the environment, and working for justice. Thus, proclamation supports the ministry, rather than ministry supporting the proclamation. Evangelism, while necessary, generates far less excitement with these friends than working for justice or some other social cause.

Certainly social ministries done in Christ's name are noble endeavors and should be part of the agenda of any Christian. But do these social values permit us to take a pass when it comes to making the gospel known? We can't help but wonder how many injustices are perpetrated because Christ is not ruling in the hearts of people who remain outside His kingdom. Societal transformation and kingdom work begin not with an emphasis on justice but with the transformation of hearts.

Now on the other side of the debate are those who see proclaiming the message of reconciliation—"that is, in Christ God was reconciling the world to himself, not counting their trespasses against them, and entrusting to us the message of reconciliation"[12]—as fulfilling the Great Commission. This ministry, they say, is conducted through proclamation—and *only* through proclamation. They say societal transformation, a good and worthy goal, comes as individuals and, eventually, whole societies are reconciled to God.

Certainly when people heed the message of reconciliation, societies tend to change for the better. As Rodney Stark noted, "The success of the West, including the rise of science, rested entirely on religious foundations, and the people who brought it about were devout Christians."[13] Anyone who would prefer the superstition, poverty, and brutality of pre-Christian Europe to the general spread of science, reason, and compassion that followed in Christianity's train just isn't paying attention.

But do those of us who believe in the authority of the Bible really need to be having this argument? Must we dichotomize social and proclamational ministry? Too many of us possess an either/or approach to the Great Commission. *Either* we seek to meet the needs of the poor and disenfranchised with gospel works, *or* we proclaim the good news with gospel words. This dichotomy between words and works is like asking which wing of an airplane is more important. Of course, it takes both wings to fly; the left and the right are both necessary.

Is it possible that we—whichever side we espouse—argue over this issue more than we actually proclaim the message of the gospel or do the works of the gospel? Perhaps we argue because we have become connoisseurs of how evangelism ought to be done rather than practitioners. Can't we agree to do more of both?

WORDS *AND* WORKS

Truth be told, the church does not have much credibility in today's world. The Mother Teresas and Shane Claibornes, sadly, are exceptional, not normative. Likewise, the Billy Grahams of this world are just as rare.

The Great Commission must be adorned by the Great Commandment, whereby Jesus instructed His followers to love God and their neighbors.[14] When the church does God's will in the world, we will produce good works—*and* disciples who will express the kingdom in word and deed. Jesus had the right balance, of course, both demonstrating and proclaiming the kingdom:

And he came to Nazareth, where he had been brought up. And as was his custom, he went to the synagogue on the Sabbath day, and he stood up to read. And the scroll of the prophet Isaiah was given to him. He unrolled the scroll and found the place where it was written,

"The Spirit of the Lord is upon me,
 because he has anointed me
 to proclaim good news to the poor.
He has sent me to proclaim liberty to the captive
 and recovering of sight to the blind,
 to set at liberty those who are oppressed,
 to proclaim the year of the Lord's favor."

And he rolled up the scroll and gave it back to the attendant and sat down. And the eyes of all in the synagogue were fixed on him. And he began to say to them, "Today this Scripture has been fulfilled in your hearing."[15]

We need both kingdom *words* and kingdom *works*. As we will discover, they flow naturally from our lives if we are experiencing God's presence.

Discussion Questions

1. Why did Christ command all of His followers to go and make disciples? While some may go as cross-cultural missionaries and others may remain in their own communities, do you think any true Christian is exempt? If so, who and why? If not, why aren't more Christians taking the command more seriously and experiencing the grace to fulfill it?

2. If God's game plan is to win the world to Himself, how active would you like to be in what He is doing? What are you likely to discover about God? About yourself?

3. Belief and obedience are linked. If you obey the Great Commission, how might your eyes be opened; and if you do not obey, how might the eyes of your faith be closed?

4. In what way do you think gospel words are necessary in sharing Christ with others? In what way do you think gospel works and acts of charity and service are necessary to make Christ known? What happens if one side of this equation is missing? Why are both essential?

5. If the Great Commission (making disciples of Christ) and the Great Commandment (loving God and neighbor) are non-negotiable for Christians, what does it look like when they are twined together and presented to the world? What would it look like for you in your own sphere of influence?

PART 2

ABIDING

IN CHRIST

6. Discovering God's Love

7. Responding to His Love

8. The Spirit: God's Abiding and Empowering Presence

9. Character: Habits of the Heart

10. Mirroring the Presence of Christ in the World

How do we begin to overcome
our fears and practice the
sacrament of evangelism?
We steep ourselves in God's love.

6) DISCOVERING GOD'S LOVE

We have challenged you to be active about evangelism even as you read this book. Of course, ultimately we are called not to be active, but to be fruitful. Fruitful disciples not only actively tell and demonstrate the gospel, but they also see people respond to both the message and the messenger. Such fruitfulness happens as they experience the immanence of God, as they practice the sacrament of evangelism. In the Upper Room Discourse, Jesus reminds the disciples (and us) about both fruitfulness and the sacramental approach to life that undergirds it:

> I am the true vine, and my Father is the vinedresser. Every branch in me that does not bear fruit he takes away, and every branch that does bear fruit he prunes, that it may bear more fruit. . . . Abide in me, and I in you. As the branch cannot bear fruit by itself, unless it abides in the vine, neither can you, unless you abide in me. I am the vine; you are the branches. Whoever abides in me and I in him, he it is that bears much fruit, for apart from me you can do nothing.[1]

Jesus says here that those who abide in Him will bear much fruit. This is the sacrament of evangelism. When we experience His nearness, we will see Him work. Jesus also says the equally important truth that if we do not abide in Him, we will not bear fruit. While we will not all produce the same quantity or type of fruit, there are no exceptions. We are *all* to abide in Christ and produce fruit. We may not all have a garrulous personality or the boldness of a used car salesman, but we are all expected to practice this sacrament. Yet the church in the West, when compared with its earlier works (not to mention the early church), in recent decades has been manifestly unfruitful. Perhaps one reason why we are not producing fruit is that we are not abiding in Christ.

BECOMING FRUITFUL

This is not in any way to discount the numerous challenges we face in evangelism today. There are many intellectual avenues for discussion down which we could travel. We might examine anthropological, sociological, geopolitical, psychological, historical, and cultural issues and factors. Social scientists can highlight demographic trends to underscore why the church is not growing. Political events and social trends, such as evangelical political involvement or the rise of the New Atheism, can influence people's receptiveness to the gospel.

There are indeed many reasons, but something still deeper underlies

C. S. Lewis wrote that pride is "worst of all the vices." Is it, or is there something even deeper?

them. We will get further, faster in this vital task not by examining the fruit but by examining the root, that is, our character. As Jesus also said, "For no good tree bears bad fruit, nor again does a bad tree bear good fruit, for each tree is known by its own fruit."[2]

In the pages that follow, we will examine some key Scriptures that give us important hints about what character qualities produce fruitfulness, and how to develop them. Then we will encourage you to cultivate both inner and outer changes so that an evangelistic lifestyle will become natural and habitual—as much a part of what it means to follow Christ as engaging in Bible study, prayer, worship, and service.

PRIDE

So let's look at ourselves at the root. Why are we so often unfruitful? Is it pride? In *Mere Christianity* C. S. Lewis wrote that pride is "worst of all the vices."[3] Is it, or is there something even deeper? Pride is certainly noxious, frightening, and destructive. Pride destroys marriages and careers, separates friends, and goads us on to waste our resources on things that don't last. Perhaps we can legitimately say that pride is at the apex of all sin. But an apex, like the top of a pyramid, is only supported by that which is much more substantial beneath it. In other words, like fruitfulness, pride comes at the end of a process.

If this is the case, what precedes and produces pride? Let's take a closer look. Suffering from pride, we try to make ourselves look better than we are. And why do we do that? Why not simply tell the truth? We do it because we are insecure in our pride. We fear that if folks really knew us as we are, as flawed and sinful people, then they might reject us. So pride involves deception—both of others and ourselves. Prideful people not only put up a pretense of being better than they are, they end up actually believing the pretense themselves. So fear precedes pride. And this insecurity permeates most human subcultures, perhaps because it is so deeply imbedded in our fallen sense of self. Think of the popular actress arrested for illegal drug use, or the CEO who's on his third marriage. Do these people, who seemingly have it all, seem secure to you?

THE GENTLE TOUCH

This insecurity even permeates our evangelical subculture, which ought to be a haven of acceptance and healing but often isn't. Christians are frequently depicted in the wider culture as hypocritically judgmental—and not wholly without reason. Interestingly, Jesus reserved some of His harshest critiques for such people.

We sometimes marginalize those who struggle to keep our rules. This is not to discount the need for personal holiness nor for the church to sometimes practice discipline among members. But often we fail to do it in the godly manner prescribed in the Bible. As Paul said, "If anyone is caught in any transgression, you who are spiritual should restore him in a spirit of gentleness."[4]

Unfortunately, too often what passes for Christian discipline lacks the gentle touch, hurting the one who is disciplined as well as our image in the world. "In certain ways, unwittingly or otherwise, we present our very worst image to the outside world, and then ask insiders to swallow a heavy dose of unreality," author Philip Yancey says. "The watching world sees Christians as strident people who try to impose their morality on others."[5]

We are harsh because we implicitly expect that everyone in our subculture—and perhaps outside it, too—should be perfect. Since no one is, this false expectation breeds pretense. We go around trying to make ourselves look better than we are. We become pharisaical, intent on keeping track of external adherence to culture-based rules such as what we wear or how we behave. But we neglect the deeper matters of the heart.

> **If we deny the riches of His love in our own communities, we will be less likely to tell others about the grace of God.**

The way we justify false notions about ourselves is reminiscent of the crowds cheering on the emperor who paraded down the street wearing not a stitch of clothing. To avoid standing out, to cover up their fears and insecurities, they embraced foolishness. Communities that deny the need for grace operate in much the same way. Their members participate in a mass delusion, which is then codified.

THE KEY

The Bible says that the antidote to this kind of fear is the love of God: "Perfect love casts out fear."[6] Perfect love doesn't just oppose fear; it obliterates it. Only God, from whom we can hide nothing, God, who fully knows us, God, who is never caught off guard by our foibles and venality, can love us thoroughly with the transformative love that casts out fear. With that kind of secure love, no wonder fear has no place in the life of the Christian who understands both God and herself.

A corollary to that verse, however, is that imperfect love breeds anxiety. Not one of us has ever been loved perfectly by another mere mortal. Francis Thompson reminds us, "Human love demands human meriting."[7] We are, each of us, saddled with a burden of anxiety by well-meaning folks who loved us as well as they could but were incapable of loving us perfectly. Of course, it gets worse. *We* have not been able to love anyone perfectly ourselves; we have saddled others with a burden of anxiety by our well-intended but deficient love.

So, if pride is at the apex of the sin pyramid, then our greatest sin, at the very base of that pyramid, is our unwillingness to receive God's love. Because we selfishly do not want to love and serve Him, we turn to surrogates in order to keep ourselves on the throne. Long ago God said to His people (people like us, who should have known better): "for my people have committed two evils: they have forsaken me, the fountain of living waters, and hewed out cisterns for themselves, broken cisterns that can hold no water."[8]

Yet God still comes to us with grace even in our darkest hours. The kingdom of God is made up of broken men and women mended by the love and mercy of God. If we deny the riches of His love in our own communities, we will be less likely to tell others about the grace of God. This grace will be so foreign to us that we will be unable to share it naturally. But if we have tasted the "perfect love that casts out fear" and are living in its light, then it will be hard to keep us quiet. So, how do we experience this perfect love?

A PICTURE OF DEVOTION

Not long ago Jerry was on an airplane, where he saw *The Notebook*, based on a novel by Nicholas Sparks. There was one incident in this film that brought tears to his eyes. But this devastating scene must be put in context. The movie begins when an old man—played by James Garner—enters the room of an elderly lady at a nursing home. The woman, played by Gena Rowlands, seems confused and standoffish. A nurse reassures her by saying that the visitor comes every day to read to her. In this moment the viewer surmises that the woman has dementia and that this kind man volunteers by reading to the residents.

The film, directed by Nick Cassavetes, alternates between scenes of this man, named Duke, reading to the woman and flashbacks to the story that he is reading. The tale in his notebook is about a young man and a young woman. She comes from an upper-class family; the young man "didn't have two dimes to rub together."[9] The woman conveys sophistication and refinement; the man, blue-collar raw. The woman has received the finest education available; the man is intelligent but untutored.

The woman has a controlling mother and father; the man's mother has died and his father is alive but distant. She lives far away and only sees him when she happens to be summering in the town where he lives. To compound the distance between them, World War II breaks out. The man goes off to fight. The woman, now working as a nurse, begins to fall for a patient more of her class and level of sophistication. Yet with all these factors working against them, the man and the woman eventually fall in love and marry.

About two-thirds of the way through the film, Jerry grasped that the old man reading the story is in fact the young man of the story, and that the old, confused woman is the young woman he fell in love with. Near the end of the film, as the shadows lengthen, the old husband and wife are eating dinner by candlelight. A single rose in a vase adorns the table. A phonograph plays the music that has graced so many of this couple's memories. Duke has diligently created this personal ambience to reach his beloved Allie, who is trapped in the deep recesses of her dementia. He finishes the story.

God's devotion is complete and unreserved, not dependent on our capacity to respond.

That is the most beautiful story she has ever heard, Allie tells Duke. She adds that it sounds so very familiar. In that moment, cognition washes across her face, and her expression changes from its default vacuity to one flush with perception. She asks her husband whether the story he has just told her is theirs.

Yes.

Then Allie, fully aware, asks how much time they have.

Last time it was about five minutes, Duke says.

She asks what any mother would: How are the children?

Duke tells her they are fine and that they visited today.

Tell them I love them, Allie requests. Duke agrees.

Then, as the music plays, she asks if they can dance. Duke stands, takes her in his arms, and they begin to move slowly to the music. Then, just as definitely as her cognition came, now it flees. Suddenly finding herself in the arms of a stranger, Allie screams. The orderlies rush into the room and must sedate the now hysterical woman. Duke stands aside, watching it all, biting his knuckles, weeping.

This is the scene that brought Jerry to tears. It illustrates something profound about all of our stories. Through the grandeur of creation, the small, unexpected gifts of everyday life, and most clearly through the sacrificial death of Christ on the cross, God is perpetually telling us about His great love for us.

Yet for most of us the default setting is a kind of spiritual dementia. Dead in our sins, we cannot hear or understand His love. Then suddenly something occurs and we see the blazing reality. In those times, we find it easy to embrace Him. But later—maybe an hour, or perhaps a day—something else happens. As easily as we fell into cognition, we fall out again.

In Duke's tears and perhaps his bleeding knuckles, we see something analogous to God's passion for us. Like the old man who visits his wife day after day, God's devotion is complete and unreserved, not dependent on our capacity to respond. His infinite love, meanwhile, has no capacity to increase, although we can grieve His Spirit by our response. The question for us is whether we will be cognizant of that love—or not.

James Garner's character, brimming with fidelity for his wife, *had* to tell her their love story again and again. If we awaken to the depths and riches of God's love for us, then we too will want to share the story of His love with others. We do this hoping that they will also awaken to the great Lover of their souls.

So how do we begin to overcome our fears and practice the sacrament of evangelism? We steep ourselves in God's love.

Discussion Questions

I. Do you think, as C. S. Lewis and St. Augustine did, that pride is the great sin? Or, is there merit for the view that rejection of God's love is the greatest sin? Explain your answer.

2. In what way do you think a growing awareness of God's presence and love in your life will make you a better witness?

3. Have you ever observed the way some Christians marginalize strugglers in their midst? Can you explain how this could produce a kind of pretence and arrogance that cloak fear and insecurity? How does this distract from a sense of the love of God in the lives of those who should be sharing that love with others? How does it confuse the message for those who might be hearing it?

4. If the poet Francis Thompson is right and "human love demands human meriting," how is God's love different? When people truly understand God's love, why do they find it attractive? How can you present the gospel to make God's love and grace clear?

5. Do you experience times when God's love seems to fade? What about times when your awareness of His presence and love are strong? What makes the difference? How does an enriched awareness of God's love for you encourage you to make that love known?

*Anyone who has walked with God—
whether for a long or short time—
knows that one's passion for Him can
chill, as in any relationship.*

7) RESPONDING TO HIS LOVE

The best thing that ever happened to Stan in college was meeting Christine through their mutual involvement with InterVarsity Christian Fellowship. Stan hadn't enjoyed a lot of dating success as a teen and young adult, to put it mildly. In his darker moments, he wasn't sure that he ever would. Like many young men who have been built for a relationship with the opposite sex, those years of physical and spiritual struggle prompted much soul-searching, many tears, and repeated prayers.

When Stan met Christine at a pizza place called Cassidy's just off campus, he immediately took note of her friendliness, intelligence, and good looks. While he was interested in someone else at the time, he made a mental note about Christine. In the weeks and months that followed, they struck up a friendship and ended up in the same campus Bible study. There he quickly came to appreciate her common sense and spiritual insight.

The relationship grew at Florida Gators football games and other campus events. They went Dutch and ate "big biscuits" together at Skeeter's, a local hangout. Once they drove to a Methodist church to hear author Robert Short discuss his book *The Gospel According to Peanuts*. Stan knew his feelings for Christine were developing and he gave her a card that praised her "unique blend of nuttiness and intellect."

He was pretty sure she felt the same way about him.

Each of us has a heart prone to wander.

Eventually Stan worked up the courage to ask Christine out on a real date. He chose a local theater, the Hippodrome, for a live performance of the play *Amadeus*, and she readily agreed. During the play (probably during the second act), Stan took another step, surreptitiously sliding his right arm around the back of her seat and lightly touching her right shoulder with his fingers. Stan held his breath—at least mentally. In God's grace and mercy, Christine laid her head on his shoulder, and the romance had officially begun.

The next several months were an intoxicating time of infatuation and fun as Stan and Christine juggled busy academic loads, InterVarsity responsibilities, and time together. Stan was the first to say, "I love you."

He was also the first to fall out of love.

COOLING OFF

As happens in all relationships, the infatuation eventually cooled, and some of the small things that hadn't seemed to matter suddenly did. Stan slowly began to wonder if he had been too hasty and if perhaps Christine wasn't "the right one" after all. But Christine hadn't gotten the memo and kept coming around. Stan, to his chagrin, actually remembers avoiding her. By God's grace, the relationship eventually recovered from Stan's fickleness, as they built their life together on foundations more enduring than puppy love.

Today Stan and Christine have a strong—if imperfect—relationship, deeper and more self-sacrificing than in their college days and yet still open to the romance and passion first awakened during that 1983 performance of *Amadeus*. A quarter of a century of marriage and three children testify that love can reawaken and persevere even after it has grown cold.

Anyone who has walked with God—whether for a long or short time—knows that one's passion for Him can chill, as in any relationship. The chilling process is a gradual one. We may hardly know it is going on. The once unquenchable desire to pray, to read the Bible, and to tell others about Him can be lost like water out of a leaky pipe. It's not that we don't love Jesus, we say to ourselves, it's just that we have something more pressing to do, or we don't want to get too "fanatical about religion."

Just as we need a gas gauge to know how much fuel we are using in a car, so we must gauge how our love for Jesus is progressing. This gauge will tell us whether we are abiding in Christ—that is, soaking in His love and growing in our love for Him—or seeing our love grow cold. If it is the latter, we cannot expect to fruitfully practice the sacrament of evangelism.

Each of us has a heart prone to wander. Jesus in fact warned that one of the key signs of the end of the age would be that "the love of many will grow cold."[1] It is good, therefore, for each of us to develop a few diagnostic questions to gauge our heart's devotion to God.

FOUR USEFUL QUESTIONS

Over the years Jerry has used four questions to help evaluate his heart for Christ. They are not a formula for everyone. In fact, they might not help you at all. Nevertheless, since all of us have the capacity to drift, a concrete diagnostic tool will probably help any serious believer. If all four don't apply to you, maybe one or two will. But the primary reason for sharing them here is simply the power of example. If they don't fit your situation, develop your own. Given our potential for struggle, each of us ought to come up with several of our own to keep track of our devotion to Christ—before our love grows cold. We need to evaluate the areas where our hearts might have a capacity to drift, and we can find out relatively easily with some well-thought-out queries.

We must keep in mind that the work of evangelism must flow not from duty or compulsion but love for Christ. This is a sacramental love, for it testifies to the nearness of God and our relational dependence upon His grace. Sacramental love, in fact, is essential for us to remind others of His presence and grace. Jesus Himself said that loving God is the most important thing any of us can do.[2]

At Whittier College, Jerry used to wonder what it would be like to be married. Jerry imagined meeting the woman with whom he would eventually tie the knot. He would imagine what it would be like to ask her out on that first date. He imagined what it would be like in the weeks and months that followed as they grew to know and love each other. Jerry imagined what it would be like to propose, and in those days of engagement, he would imagine what it would be like to make plans for their life together.

Then Jerry thought about what the wedding day might be like—perhaps standing with his brothers and brother-in-law and his closest friends at the front of the church. The organ music would swell, and his bride would come up the aisle with her father. He would imagine the pastor asking them to say their vows and hear him pronounce them husband and wife. Next he would imagine the minister introducing them to the congregation as Mr. and Mrs. Root, with their families and friends breaking into applause. Then Jerry would imagine leaving the church altar behind and starting down the aisle to begin a new life with his bride.

> **If we expect spouse, children, career, friends, or hobbies to do for us what only God can do, then we are bound for disappointment.**

But then Jerry would stop, fearing that this was the most likely moment that Jesus would return, cutting their new life together short. The sinking feeling this thought produced used to bother him horribly. So he came up with his first diagnostic question:

I. "If Jesus came back this moment, would I be disappointed?"

The fear that Jesus might return right after his wedding made Jerry wonder, rightly, if he was beginning to long for married life more than for the Bridegroom. For you the competition with Christ's love might be something different, such as wealth, children, or travel. Such things, when put in their proper perspective, are usually not bad in themselves. The things that begin to steal our devotion to Christ are often things we in fact *should* long for. They are most often good gifts that contribute to our happiness in this world.

Nevertheless, these relatively good and important things can never adequately function as replacements for God in our lives. Marriage is fulfilling but cannot fully satisfy. Having children is a blessing, but they cannot meet your deepest needs. Building a career you love may be purposeful, but it cannot guarantee satisfaction. Only God, who made us for Himself, can ultimately fulfill.

If we expect spouse, children, career, friends, or hobbies to do for us what only God can do, then we are bound for disappointment. Sinful and broken as we are, we may even begin to project that disappointment onto the people in our life—with long-term deleterious results. The problem, of course, is not with them; it's with us. It was our misdirected affections that created and sustain the problem.

When we ask "If Jesus came back today, would I be disappointed?" we do not have to beat ourselves up if something appears on our mental computer screens that rivals our affections for God. This question is supposed to reveal such things, so that we can do something about them, not prove our perfection or produce guilt. With this knowledge in place, we can begin to set the affections of our hearts on God first. If we put first things first, we will enjoy second things in their proper places. But if we put *second* things first, we will lose out on both first *and* second things.

We are not less spiritual for asking this diagnostic question and dealing with any rivals that may emerge. Having the courage to ask means we are maturing in Christ. And keeping our affections first on Christ will make us more credible in personal evangelism.

We will be calling others to the One we have learned to love so deeply—the One who loves all whom He has uniquely created.

The second diagnostic question is almost the flip side of the first.

2. "Can I say thank You to God in the midst of my current circumstances?"

Note that we do not ask whether we can thank God *for* our circumstances. Some of us face horrible situations, at times the consequences of our own or others' bad choices. We do not have to give thanks for the fruits of dysfunction or sin. Asking this question tests our hearts to see if we can thank God even though our world may be crumbling around us. Why? Because He is enough. As Habakkuk said:

> Though the fig tree should not blossom,
> nor fruit be on the vines,
> the produce of the olive fail
> and the fields yield no food,
> the flock be cut off from the fold
> and there be no herd in the stalls,
> yet I will rejoice in the Lord;
> I will take joy in the God of my salvation.[3]

If we are tethering our hearts and expectations to anything that can be taken from us, then we are setting ourselves up for disappointment. If we have devoted our hearts to those things that moth and rust destroy and thieves break in and steal, we will be devastated on the day when their true nature is revealed and our idolatry has been uncovered. But, in the act of saying thank You to God when such a day arises, we declare, like Habakkuk, that God is enough. In this fallen world, those who know that the worst the world can throw at us cannot diminish our eternal fulfillment carry a special authority.

If you ask this question and struggle because something comes up on your mental computer screen, you are not an unspiritual person. Yes, you would be unspiritual if you let matters stay that way. Soon your heart would drift from God in bitterness and disappointment, as happens to so many. Asking the question, however, makes it possible for you to wrestle with real life issues and in that place discover the transcending triumph of Christ in your life. This sacramental realization will better equip you for the sacrament of evangelism.

The third question arises out of 1 John 4:20, where the apostle observes that it is difficult to say that we love God, whom we haven't seen, if we do not love our brother or sister, whom we have. Here then is the question:

3. "Am I out of sorts with someone?"

Is there a broken relationship that I am responsible for in which estrangement exists? We are not talking about those relationships in which you have done all you can but the other person refuses to reconcile (even God has some of those). We mean those broken relationships you *could* mend, if you desired. The Scriptures warn that your love for God may grow cold if you don't do something, by His grace, to fix them. Prayerfully applying this question opens our hearts to discovering those relationships that require mending.

If you ask this question and a person or situation comes to mind, again, you are not unspiritual—unless you do nothing to address the problem. Engaging in the sacrament of evangelism and explaining to those around us that "God was in Christ reconciling the world to himself" are difficult, to say the least, if we are unwilling to be reconciled to a brother or sister. This state of affairs will jeopardize our devotion to Christ and sap our passion to tell others about Him.

4. "Do you love Me?"

The fourth question also comes from Scripture. The night Jesus was betrayed, Peter had spoken boldly, perhaps too boldly. He boasted that while he was not confident that the other disciples would stand with Christ in the hour of testing, he had no doubts about his own devotion through thick or thin. Jesus, knowing Peter's heart better than he did, told Peter that he would deny Him three times. Incredulous, Peter was convinced of his impetuous boasts and utterly unaware of the drift occurring in his own heart. The story of what happened that night has been told through the ages.[4] Peter did, in fact, deny Christ and cursed when asked if he knew Him. He had let down his best friend in His hour of need. What a crushing burden for Peter, who went out and wept bitterly! And yet who among us has not also denied Him at one time or another?

Imagine looking into the eyes of Jesus as He asks, "Do you love Me?"

On the morning of Christ's resurrection, the angel appeared to Mary Magdalene at the empty tomb, announcing that Jesus was risen from the dead. The angel said Mary must tell the disciples. Then he specified that Mary must make sure she told *Peter*.[5] It is an incredible comment. Peter was drowning in guilt and remorse, and the Lord wanted him to know that His grace was sufficient. This sufficiency includes not just the wayward apostle but all the Peters of this world who have denied Him.

Dorothy Sayers, in her essay "The Triumph of Easter,"[6] observes that it was too bad Judas didn't stick around, for even his sin and betrayal of Christ were not beyond God's power to forgive. In this context, the fourth question grows out of the resurrected Christ's encounter with Peter.[7]

Jesus asks a simple question: "Peter, do you love Me?"

Put your own name in the question as you imagine looking into the eyes of Jesus, who loves you with an everlasting love. It is overwhelming to imagine what that moment must have been like for Peter . . . what it is like for any of us when we come to similar turning points in life. Jesus used the word *agape* for love when He asked, "Peter, do you love Me?" It is the New Testament word that so often speaks of that unique, God-like love that exhibits itself in acts of charity and mercy, love and grace.

Peter, remarkably self-aware, responds, "Yes, Lord; I love You." But he does not use Jesus' word *agape;* instead, he uses the word *phileo*, which speaks of friendship. In essence, Peter answers, "Lord, I like You a lot; we are friends." Remarkably, Jesus does not chide Peter. He does not say, "Peter, if that's the best you can do, go away and don't return until you can be as devoted to Me as I am to you." No, Christ accepted Peter and the level of love he could honestly give and even commissioned him into service with the words "Tend My lambs."

A second time, Jesus asks, "Peter, do you love Me?" Peter

answers, "Yes, Lord; I like You." Jesus replies, "Shepherd My sheep." Again the commission comes after Peter's affirmation of imperfect love. A third time Jesus asks the question, this time using Peter's word: "Peter, do you like Me a lot?" Peter answers, "Lord, You know all things; You know that I like You." Here again, Jesus commissions Peter to service: "Tend My sheep."

If Jesus were to ask us that same question, would we even be able to rise to the level of Peter's "Lord, I like you a lot"? Sometimes the best we can do is prayerfully reply, "Lord, I *want* to love You." Sometimes our prayer is more desperate still, turning into a "Lord, I *want* to want to love You."

But God hears even these prayers and turns the "Lord, I want to want to love You" into a "Lord, I want to love You." Sometimes, on the best of days, we may even say to God, "Lord, I love You." Whatever the case, all ministry for Christ, and especially personal evangelism, ought to flow from our devotion to Christ.

Asking these questions—or others like them—will help any believer respond in love to the One who is present and mediating grace.

Discussion Questions

1. As evidence of the frailty of our humanity, we can be fickle in our relationships—marriages, families, friendships, and so forth. Often these relationships need attention and repair. So when your love for God begins to cool, what do you do to heat it up again?

2. Which of the four questions presented in this chapter did you find most helpful in gauging your own devotion to Christ? Why was that particular question so helpful?

3. Think of another question you want to add to this list. Why would it be helpful to you?

4. If Jesus looked you in the eye right now and asked, "Do you love Me?" how would you answer? Would you be secure enough in relationship with Him to give an honest assessment? Are you willing to make such an honest assessment of these things to yourself or to close and caring friends? If you were standing before Jesus right now (and you are no less proximate to Him in this moment than Peter was to Him at the shores of Galilee), how would you ask Him to help you love Him more?

5. Why is it so important to share the gospel with others out of an honest, rich, and growing love for Christ?

Sometimes we simply have to

trust that the Spirit is working

even when we do not see the results.

8) THE SPIRIT: GOD'S ABIDING AND EMPOWERING PRESENCE

When Jerry was a youth pastor in southern California, he and others on staff would take the high school youth group down into the Mexicali Valley to do mission work. Mexicali, on Mexico's Baja Peninsula, is the northernmost city in Latin America. One year Jerry led a group into a village named Jalisco. Reports filed by previous teams said that response in Jalisco was virtually non-existent. The new team had its work cut out for it and began to pray hard for the Spirit's leading.

The plan was for team members to sleep on the floor of a church in nearby El Centro. In the morning they worked on a vacation Bible school ministry for the village and put together the evening worship service. After an early lunch in El Centro, the team would head to Jalisco. Afternoons were spent evangelizing children. The team would leave the village to eat a brown bag dinner before returning for evening worship services under a lean-to attached to the house of a local believer, Jesus Alverez.

In El Centro the team was assigned two male translators, in addition to two female translators who were already part of the ministry. The first male was a very elderly man named Prudentio. Jerry worried that the trip would be too taxing for him and that he might even die. The other was nineteen-year-old Jose, who had only recently come to Christ. Before his conversion Jose had been a gangbanger in East Los Angeles. Jerry felt very discouraged. After preparing and praying so diligently, he wondered why the team had not received mature Christian translators who had walked with Christ longer than Jose but who were not as decrepit as Prudentio.

The first afternoon in Jalisco seemed to go well. All of the children came to an open field. The team played games, did crafts, and shared Bible stories and testimonies with them. At the end of the afternoon, the team asked them to invite family members to join them at Jesus Alverez's lean-to for an evening service. But when the team returned after dinner, members were discouraged to find that only the children, a very old woman, and two teenage girls showed up. Nothing seemed to be going right. Where were the adults? Would they have to add one more disappointing report to the Jalisco file at the end of the week? Would the village remain forsaken by God?

A SURPRISING OUTCOME

The next day, all the kids were eager to play with the high schoolers from Los Estados Unidos. Jerry was still frustrated and asked the female translators to take charge of the children's activities. He decided to take Prudentio and Jose to personally invite all of the men to that evening's scheduled meeting. Worried that the trek might prove too difficult for Prudentio, he nevertheless led the translators door to door.

That afternoon Jerry was struck by how the men they visited gave them their attention. They were particularly responsive to Prudentio and Jose, but Jerry didn't know what to make of it. Jerry, Prudentio, and Jose spent the entire afternoon visiting the men. They returned just in time to leave the village for dinner.

When the three returned for the service at Jesus Alverez's house, none of the children were in sight. The two teenage girls and the old woman were also absent. To their surprise, however, every man in the village had shown up. The entire congregation was made up of men. After a few songs, Jose spoke about how he came to know Christ and was rescued from the gangs of East Los Angeles. The men listened with deep interest. They were clearly impressed at God's power to transform young Jose's life and make him a follower of Jesus.

When Prudentio spoke, their interest intensified. Jerry hadn't realized how much Hispanic culture respected age. Prudentio's long walk with Jesus, his knowledge of the Scriptures, and his testimony to the faithfulness of Christ over the years broke through. Every one of the men gave his heart to Christ.

Despite Jerry's initial misgivings, the Holy Spirit knew what He was about when He provided those two beloved interpreters. They were exactly what the ministry to Jalisco needed.

The next evening, *everyone* in the village showed up. All of the men were there; all of their wives; all of the teenagers, both the girls and the boys; and all of the children. And so it went for the rest of the week as an unexpected revival broke out. Soon teams from Jalisco were doing evangelism in other villages in the valley.

THE SPIRIT'S WORKS

While we may experience many manifestations of the Spirit's work in our lives, probably the most common will be how He will walk with us to share God's love and grace with others. The Scriptures are explicit that abiding in Christ will lead to Spirit-led evangelistic fruitfulness.

Jesus makes an explicit connection between the life of witness and the ministry of the Holy Spirit.

As Jerry's experience in Jalisco shows, the Spirit's presence and power can accomplish more in evangelism than our most diligent efforts. Jesus also said, "Truly, truly, I say to you, whoever believes in me will also do the works that I do; and greater works than these will he do, because I am going to the Father."[1] What could He have meant by this remarkable statement? There are several possibilities. He could have meant that:

- whatever miracles Jesus did, His disciples would do as well.
- His disciples would do greater works by virtue of their sheer number.
- His followers would do greater works in the sense that, as sinners, we innately lack the capability to do anything at all.

What we do know is that these greater works (however we understand *greater*) are possible because Jesus (1) modeled for His disciples how to do ministry[2] and (2) would equip them with what they needed to accomplish the task.

In the upper room, Jesus told His disciples,

> And I will ask the Father, and he will give you another Helper, to be with you forever, even the Spirit of truth, whom the world cannot receive, because it neither sees him nor knows him. You know him, for he dwells with you and will be in you.
>
> I will not leave you as orphans; I will come to you. Yet a little while and the world will see me no more, but you will see me. Because I live, you also will live. In that day you will know that I am in my Father, and you in me, and I in you. Whoever has my commandments and keeps them, he it is who loves me. And he who loves me will be loved by my Father, and I will love him and manifest myself to him. . . . If anyone loves me, he will keep my word, and my Father will love him, and we will come to him and make our home with him."[3]

As Jesus got His marching orders from the Father,[4] now the church would get her marching orders from the Holy Spirit. This instruction, though less developed, is echoed in the last words Jesus spoke to His disciples before the ascension: "But you will receive power when the Holy Spirit has come upon you, and you will be my witnesses in Jerusalem and in all Judea and Samaria, and to the end of the earth."[5] Here Jesus makes an explicit connection between the life of witness and the ministry of the Holy Spirit. Perhaps believers who do not experience evangelistic fruitfulness are missing out on the power of the Holy Spirit.

HIS BAPTISM AND PRESENCE

Scripture uses different terms to describe the presence and ministry of the Holy Spirit in the life of the believer.

Baptism by (or in) the Holy Spirit.

John the Baptist said, "I have baptized you with water, but he will baptize you with the Holy Spirit."[6] John's baptism purified on the outside, but Jesus' baptism would purify from within through the ministry of the Holy Spirit. Later, the apostle Paul says, "For we were all baptized by one Spirit into one body."[7] The word *baptized* literally means "to place into." The verb is in the aorist tense, which speaks of completed action in past time. The baptism by the Holy Spirit is *completed*. It is the act of the Spirit of God to place the new believer into the body of Christ. This happens once, the moment we come to Christ.

The filling of the Holy Spirit.

This filling is not to be confused with the once-for-all baptism of the Spirit. The filling of the Spirit is instead the animating power behind a holy life. First, Paul tells the Christians at Ephesus to "put off your old self, which belongs to your former manner of life and is corrupt through deceitful desires, and to be renewed in the spirit of your minds, and to put on the new self, created after the likeness of God in true righteousness and holiness."[8] Later, he says, "Look carefully then how you walk, not as unwise but as wise, making the best use of the time, because the days are evil."[9] The word translated *carefully* is the same word from which we get the English *acrobat*. It takes balance.

Only the Holy Spirit can bring such balance. And how are we filled with Him? Paul says we must "understand what the will of the Lord is . . . be filled with the Spirit."[10] *Be filled* is an imperative expressed in a passive voice, present tense. In essence, the text is telling believers to let it be done to them; let the Holy Spirit's filling come upon you. In other words, stop doing whatever is preventing you from experiencing the filling of the Holy Spirit.

Campus Crusade offers a simple but powerful approach called Spiritual Breathing. First, believers are to *exhale,* or confess their sin (or sins). "If we confess our sins, he is faithful and just to forgive us our sins and to cleanse us from all unrighteousness."[11] The word translated *confess* means "to say the same thing." We must tell God the very things He knows about us already. We do not need to (and in fact cannot) hide anything from Him. He not only knows it long before we have confessed but has already forgiven it in Christ.

We need to keep in mind that all believers are called to serve in some areas even when they do not have the matching spiritual gift.

To *inhale,* on the other hand, is simply to ask God to fill us with His Spirit. We can be confident that He will do so: "And this is the confidence that we have toward him, that if we ask anything according to his will he hears us. And if we know that he hears us in whatever we ask, we know that we have the requests that we have asked of him."[12]

HIS WORK IN INDIVIDUALS

So the baptism and filling of the Spirit are normative for Christians. But God does not create unique individuals only to call them into a uniformity of existence. We have a wide range of differences relative to gender, personality, ethnicity, culture, and so forth. Further, God distributes unique gifts to His children. The Bible encourages us to employ those gifts in unique ways, even in the service of a shared purpose.

Scripture lists many gifts of the Holy Spirit, each given for the common good in order that God's people may fulfill God's purposes in the world: [13]

- Romans 12:6–15 says God has given gifts of prophecy, serving, teaching, exhorting, giving, leading, and mercy.
- 1 Corinthians 12:7–11 lists wisdom, knowledge, faith, healing, miracles, discerning of spirits, speaking in tongues, and interpretation of tongues.
- The Old Testament points us to several people who were filled with the Spirit to do artistic work[14] or to do mighty feats of strength.[15]

We need to keep in mind that all believers are called to serve in some areas even when they do not have the matching spiritual gift. For example, all must give even though only some have the actual gift of giving. Not all have the gift of evangelism, yet all are called to engage in evangelism in whatever part of the world God has assigned them. No believer should ever use his or her giftedness or lack thereof as an excuse to avoid those activities all are commanded to do.

The Scriptures also teach about the *fruit* of the Spirit: "But the fruit of the Spirit is love, joy, peace, patience, kindness, goodness, faithfulness, gentleness, self-control."[16] This fruit speaks of Christlike attitudes that should develop in our lives. We should see them as we graciously employ our spiritual gifts for others. This fruit will point others to the presence of God as we participate in the purposes of God. As Paul said, "But thanks be to God, who in Christ always leads us in triumphal procession, and through us spreads the fragrance of the knowledge of him everywhere."[17]

When you are filled with the Holy Spirit, at times you will sense a prompting by the Spirit to tell another person about Jesus. These promptings will likely have no audible voice, but nonetheless the impulse will be strong, clear, and persistent. When you respond to this prompting, the results, as in Jalisco, may be beyond anything you can imagine.

TRUSTING THAT HE'S WORKING

But sometimes we simply have to trust that the Spirit is working even when we do not see the results. One summer during his college years, Jerry was out of work and concerned about paying for his tuition. The local YMCA asked if he would be willing to run its summer day camp and a weeklong residential camp in the mountains. Feeling prompted by the Holy Spirit, Jerry replied that he would direct the camps if the YMCA would allow the counselors to tell Bible stories and let him share the gospel at the park sleepover at week's end. Jerry also requested permission to share the gospel at the final campfire of the residential camp. Most YMCA program staff were Christians, and they readily granted permission. Even so, Jerry did not receive permission to do any follow-up.

During the summer, Jerry and the counselors saw more than five hundred young people trust Christ, including about 120 around the campfire the last night at the residential camp. Later Jerry often wondered whatever became of those kids and prayed that God would watch after His own.

Years later, Jerry was a youth pastor in a Los Angeles suburb. One evening a new boy came to the Bible study, invited by a school friend. After the meeting Jerry introduced himself. The teenager, whose name was Mike, said his family had recently moved to the suburbs and was looking for a church. Mike said he was a Christian, so Jerry asked for the story of how he came to faith.

Mike said that years before he had attended a YMCA camp in the mountains. The last night his dad had driven up to join him. His family was leaving for a vacation the next day and wanted to get away before the Y buses would get him back to the city. Mike said that the camp director stood up around the campfire and shared the gospel, and that he and his dad both trusted in Christ. Mike's family started going to church, and soon his mother and two sisters also came to faith. Jerry's heart nearly skipped a beat.

"Mike," Jerry asked, "what was the name of that camp?"

"Little Green Valley Y-Camp."

"What was the name of the YMCA you were a part of that took you to the camp?"

"It was the Southeast Y in Huntington Park, in Los Angeles."

Jerry choked up as he told Mike that he had been the director of the camp and had spoken that night around the campfire. Mike and Jerry both thanked God for allowing them to connect the dots in their two stories. Jerry was overwhelmed with gratitude that God had given him every reason to believe that the others who had given their lives to Christ that summer were also being looked after by a God who loved them. Whether we ever similarly discover in this life the results of our sacramental evangelism, we can rest assured that the work of the Holy Spirit who indwells us will go on.

Discussion Questions

1. Have you seen God work in a situation unexpectedly? Describe the circumstances.

2. You were baptized by the Holy Spirit and placed into the body of Christ when you trusted Christ to forgive you of your sins and made Him your Savior and Lord. Has it sunk in that God wants you to know continually Christ's presence and the Holy Spirit's power each day? How might a more robust awareness of the Holy Spirit's presence increase your confidence in sharing the gospel?

3. Being filled with the Holy Spirit is the normal state for Christians, and living contrary to God's purposes quenches the Spirit's work and limits your effective service for Christ. Is anything preventing you from confessing your sins to the God who loves you so deeply and asking Him to fill you with His Holy Spirit right now?

4. Ask the Spirit of God to open your eyes to people in your world He is already wooing to Himself. Who might they be? Have you considered that your present concern for them might be directly linked to the Holy Spirit's prompting in your life right now?

5. Pray that God will work through you to reach others in ways that could only be attributed to Him. How would your own faith be encouraged if you saw Him work through you this way?

The sacramental evangelist should strive for the pillars of virtue that lead to evangelistic fruitfulness.

9) CHARACTER: HABITS OF THE HEART

We have met the apostle Peter in his worst moment—denying his Lord to a servant girl during the night of Jesus' arrest. We have also seen him, mere weeks later, boldly preaching the gospel in the teeth of powerful opposition, knowing that God was with him. It was something the suddenly bold apostle and leader would do repeatedly, whatever the cost. As Luke reports in the book of Acts,

> And the high priest questioned them, saying, "We strictly charged you not to teach in this name, yet here you have filled Jerusalem with your teaching, and you intend to bring this man's blood upon us." But Peter and the apostles answered, "We must obey God rather than men. The God of our fathers raised Jesus, whom you killed by hanging him on a tree. God exalted him at his right hand as Leader and Savior, to give repentance to Israel and forgiveness of sins. And we are witnesses to these things, and so is the Holy Spirit, whom God has given to those who obey him."

... They beat them and charged them not to speak in the name of Jesus, and let them go. Then they left the presence of the council, rejoicing that they were counted worthy to suffer dishonor for the name. And every day, in the temple and from house to house, they did not cease teaching and preaching Jesus as the Christ.[1]

The sacrament of evangelism does many things in our lives. It makes us aware of the God who is here, both in our lives and in the lives of those we attempt to reach with the gospel. It makes us praying people. It forces us to rely on the Holy Spirit as we walk with Him by faith. But it does even more. It makes us more mature. It deepens and thickens our character.

Peter went almost overnight from being a cringing coward to a courageous truth-teller. Peter's character, worked over patiently by Jesus during three years of ministry and training, suddenly bore fruit when the time came to stand up in the power of the Spirit.

And in fact Jesus had told Peter that he would die a martyr's death. Imagine if *you* knew how you were going to die. Would this knowledge lessen your *joie de vivre* as you awaited the end? Yet we have no subsequent record of Peter's fear and foreboding. To the contrary, Peter the sacramental evangelist became a pillar of the church, joyously taking the gospel throughout the ancient world, unafraid of the consequences.[2] Here was a man sold out for God, a man whose character had been transformed.

PETER'S CHANGED CHARACTER

Peter knew what it was like to grow in the presence of God. In this chapter we will examine Peter to see what a changed character looks like, because this is one of the hallmarks of the sacrament of evangelism. People who grow in character are effective and fruitful.

Here is what Peter said about it:

> Make every effort to supplement your faith with virtue, and virtue with knowledge, and knowledge with self-control, and self-control with steadfastness, and steadfastness with godliness, and godliness with brotherly affection, and brotherly affection with love. For if these qualities are yours and are increasing, they keep you from being ineffective or unfruitful in the knowledge of our Lord Jesus Christ. For whoever lacks these qualities is so nearsighted that he is blind, having forgotten that he was cleansed from his former sins. Therefore, brothers, be all the more diligent to make your calling and election sure, for if you practice these qualities you will never fall. For in this way there will be richly provided for you an entrance into the eternal kingdom of our Lord and Savior Jesus Christ.[3]

Courage is endurance, fortitude, and staying power.

This is a remarkable statement, full of assurances for the Christian. Among other things, Peter provides the recipients of this letter (including us) a list of desired character qualities: faith, virtue, knowledge, self-control, steadfastness, godliness, brotherly affection, and love. Then he adds, "If these qualities are yours and are increasing, they keep you from being ineffective or unfruitful in the knowledge of our Lord Jesus Christ."

The word translated as *virtue* here is the same one used in the Greek texts of the philosophers and sages of classical times. Peter knew his culture and how to use the best from it in the cause of the gospel. Virtue, in that era, was seen as an integrated whole made up of *courage, temperance, justice,* and *wisdom*—the four cardinal virtues.[4] If a person lacked any of these four qualities, he or she could not claim to have achieved virtue.

Peter made the further connection between virtue, or moral excellence, and fruitfulness. As we have seen, being able to reproduce the life of Christ in others is a core element of fruitfulness. The sacramental evangelist, therefore, should strive for the pillars of virtue that lead to evangelistic fruitfulness. We will examine them in the balance of this chapter.

THE HABIT OF COURAGE

The ancients saw courage not as a single act of bravery but as a habit of life. One act of heroism does not make a person courageous any more than one act of forbearance makes a person temperate, or one act of justice makes one just. Achieving these qualities requires a transformation of the life patterns that shape character.

Courage, then, must be defined as the habitual ability to suffer pain and hardship; it is endurance, fortitude, and staying power. Courage is the habit of saying yes to right action even at risk of pain or loss. Courage never gives up. Courage sticks with a task until it is done. Courage faces one's fears and does the right thing in spite of them.

Courage means we can look honestly at our flaws that need to be pruned if we are to bear more fruit; courage can hear criticism and grow from it rather than wither from its heat. Courage also makes it possible to look at the potential pain and risks and endure in service to Christ. It was courage, coupled with the grace of Christ, that allowed a person such as Peter, who had once failed badly, to endure until the end. According to tradition, and as Jesus had predicted, Peter was eventually crucified (upside down) for his Lord. And it is courage that will make each of us faithful to our evangelistic task.

THE HABIT OF TEMPERANCE

The second virtue we need for evangelistic fruitfulness, temperance, is the habitual ability to resist the enticement of immediate pleasure in order to gain a greater though more remote good. As courage is the ability to say yes to right action in the teeth of pain, so too, temperance is the ability to say no to wrong action even in the jaws of pleasure.

Temperance is one of the chief characteristics of maturity. Yet temperance, we can easily observe today, is little seen and even less praised. The words "temperance movement" conjure up sepia-tinted images of quaint Prohibition-era social restrictions. They do not encourage us to be temperate. We know of too many people who choose the fleeting pleasures of infidelity over a solid marriage, demonstrating nothing if not a lack of temperance.

Everyone knows how children will make any kind of compromise to get a treat. Jerry developed a plan to teach temperance to his kids. Often upon coming home from work, he would bring them some kind of simple surprise, maybe a small piece of candy, perhaps a mint or a butterscotch tightly wrapped in yellow cello-phane. Jerry would tell them, "You can have this piece of candy now, or I will take you to the store and buy you a toy tomorrow for ten dollars." When Jerry first began this experiment, his children—incredibly, it seems—always chose the candy. Finally the oldest, Jeremy, decided to take the toy. As the other children chomped on their candy, they looked at Jeremy as if he were crazy. But their expressions changed the next day when he came home with the toy. Over time, each began to see the benefits of temperance.

Temperance is not the refusal of pleasure but rather the will-ingness to choose the greater, and often longer-term, good over the lesser, and often immediate, pleasure. Temperance applies whether the issue is candy vs. a toy, illicit sexual pleasures vs. one's marriage, or pursuing the accolades of others vs. doing what God requires. In fact, temperance is more a developed skill than a personality trait; it comes from discernment that is manifest in good choices.

Peter says that temperance leads to a fruitful life. Sometimes we Christians show a lack of temperance as we fatten ourselves on the short-term benefits of Bible study and church business, while the world is starving to know the love of God. We are trad-ing a long-term good—the growth of the kingdom—for short-term benefits that will not last if we do not apply them. Those who develop the virtue of temperance, however, learn how to set aside personal pleasure to invite others to the table of God's grace.

THE HABIT OF JUSTICE

Plato, Aristotle, Augustine, and other giants of the ancient world saw justice as integral to moral excellence. In *The Repub-lic*, Plato has Socrates define the concept thusly:

Justice, which directly applies to social issues, nevertheless implies superior character and intelligence in those who are committed to it. Injustice, however, means deficiency in both respects. Therefore, just men are superior in character and intelligence and are more effective in action. As injustice implies ignorance, stupidity and badness, it cannot be superior in character and intelligence. A just man is wiser because he acknowledges the principle of limit.

Unlimited self-assertion is not a source of strength for any group organized for common purpose, Unlimited desire and claims lead to conflicts.

Life of just man is better and happier. There is always some specific virtue in everything, which enables it to work well. If it is deprived of that virtue, it works badly. The soul has specific functions to perform. When it performs its specific functions, it has specific excellence or virtue. If, it is deprived of its peculiar virtue, it cannot possibly do its work well. It is agreed that the virtue of the soul is justice. The soul which is more virtuous or in other words more just is also the happier soul. Therefore, a just man lives happy. A just soul, in other words a just man, lives well; an unjust cannot.[5]

Peter does not use the specific word *justice*, but he does employ a number of terms that form a composite that constitutes justice. Peter's words are "godliness," "brotherly affection," and "love." Each demonstrates concern for the welfare of others—a concern that is emphasized and underscored when the words are used together.

Justice may be defined as the habit (there's that word again) of being concerned for the general welfare of one's society. It secures and protects natural rights for others; it is fair; and it renders to others their due. To render to others their due is not merely to punish the evildoer. It also demands the praise and proper treatment of the well doer. Justice recognizes our responsibility to others. It is action-oriented. As Augustine remarked, "Charity is no substitute for justice withheld."[6]

Embedded in justice is the idea that if I do not assume my responsibility to serve others, my own happiness will suffer. Peter knew this. Fruitfulness occurs when love, godliness, and brotherly affection characterize a believer's life.

THE HABIT OF WISDOM

Peter does not use the commonest word for wisdom, that is, *sophia*. Rather, he uses *ginosko*, which describes experiential knowledge, as opposed to skill (*episteme*) or mere intellectual knowledge (*oida*). Peter's word choice supports the traditional understanding of wisdom and knowledge as practically applied. Wisdom is the habit (yes, *habit*) of being careful about one's decisions; it seeks counsel and advice. As Proverbs 15:22 states, "Without counsel plans fail, but with many advisers they succeed."

Wisdom grows out of the commonsense recognition that we do not know very much and desperately need to know more. While the pursuit of knowledge is one of our society's highest ideals, one of the first things any honest person must admit is that we cannot know everything. The Widener Library at Harvard College has more than six million volumes. The Bodleian Library at Oxford University has about 130 miles of shelf space. We cannot possibly absorb it all. Yet this is no reason for the wise person to give up learning.

And we must strive to know more even about the areas in which we feel adequate. Augustine also understood that wisdom takes work, saying, "Patience is the companion of wisdom."[7] The pursuit of wisdom will not allow our current understanding to remain stagnant. Truths we know can be known more deeply still; and they can be applied to fresh challenges unanticipated by the past.

Wisdom not only is always right—it is always relevant. This is certainly true for those of us engaged in the sacrament of evangelism. We know that the Savior who goes with us and meets us when we get there does not change: "Jesus Christ is the same yesterday and today and forever."[8] But each individual to whom we go is unique. His or her needs, personality, and history are particular. We need wisdom to respond sensitively and appropriately to each person created by God and scarred by the fall.

Peter says when we possess these four characteristics of virtue—courage, temperance, justice, and wisdom—and see them increasing, we will become effective and fruitful. And the converse is also true: If we are not growing in these areas, then our evangelistic fruitfulness may be hindered. Perhaps, then, when the church becomes unfruitful, we should encourage the development of virtue. The body of Christ must possess increasing virtue if we are to fulfill Christ's mission.

If we do, we also will be more like Him. That is the subject of chapter 10.

Discussion Questions

1. What did you learn about courage from 2 Peter 1:1–11 and this chapter? How might courage help you share the gospel with others more effectively?

2. What did you learn about temperance? How might the cultivation of temperance make you more useful and fruitful in telling others about God's love and forgiveness in Christ?

3. What did you learn about justice? How might justice make you a better witness for Christ? We owe it to others to pass on what we have so freely received of God's love and grace. Have you considered that failure to share the gospel may be an injustice, and that faithfulness in sharing with others may be an act of justice? How might this be so? How does telling others about Jesus render to them their due?

4. What did you learn about wisdom? How might growth in wisdom make you a better witness for Christ?

5. Is it possible that we are not availing ourselves of God's grace to grow in character? If so, why? What can be done to help Christians cultivate the qualities that will make them more useful and fruitful?

The sacramental evangelist

should not merely experience

God in her daily life,

but reflect Him to others.

10) MIRRORING THE PRESENCE OF CHRIST IN THE WORLD

Years ago a man walked up to Jerry with a desperate look on his face. "Jerry," the man said in a defeated voice, "please pray for me. I am the only Christian in my workplace, and I am miserable." So Jerry put his hands on the man's shoulders and intoned, "Lord, look on my brother here and see how miserable he is. Please take him out of this world and on to heaven, for he isn't doing You a lick of good here."

Stunned, the man knocked Jerry's hands off of his shoulders, exclaiming, "What are you praying?!!?" Jerry then replied, "I am praying for you to go home to heaven because you are doing no heavenly good here. You are just occupying space." Ouch. Sometimes—often, perhaps—the truth hurts.

God has called us not to occupy space until the Lord calls us home but to join Him in His work in the world. If you are the only

Christian in your workplace, in your neighborhood, or on your softball team, don't be miserable. Think and pray strategically. Instead of moping, you can discover what God has planned for good in your world and in your life as you point out His presence to others.

The sacrament of evangelism means more than merely looking for Christ in the world He created and loves. It also means letting Christ, who is present *in* you, manifest His presence *through* you. First John 4:17 (NIV) says that "in this world we are like him." People can't see Jesus in the flesh, but they can see us. And if they see us, they can see Him, if our imperfect but graced lives are tuned to His.

REFLECTING HIM

The sacramental evangelist should not merely *experience* God in her daily life, but reflect Him to others. Just as a dirty window must be cleaned to reveal what is on the other side, so too the sacramental evangelist needs to ensure her own life is clean so that Christ will shine through her. We are little windows to Christ.

Or, to change the metaphor a bit, we are mirrors, reflecting Him to those around us, those for whom we are earnestly praying to know God's love and grace. But how do we, unholy and broken mirrors that we are, reflect our holy Lord? How is such a thing possible when we are so unlike Him?

It is certainly not a matter of pulling ourselves up by our moral bootstraps. We cannot reflect Jesus by trying to improve ourselves. In that case, all that people will ever see is more of us, not more of Him. Most religions tell us to clean up our lives, to work harder, to do more. Even if we somehow find a way to obey all the laws and regulations that well-intended religion can throw at us, we cannot, by so doing, get beyond ourselves. Such obedience, even if done sincerely, is likely not to build our humility, but our pride. Truly, as Isaiah 64:6 (NIV) reminds us, "All our righteous acts are like filthy rags."

How do we deal with this ever-present filth, so that people see not us, but Him? The answer lies not in trying to make ourselves similar to Jesus, but in coming to the end of ourselves. As John the Baptist said, "He must increase, but I must decrease."[1] He must increase; we must decrease. We must emphasize the differences. The differences are what will make it possible for your friends and neighbors to see Jesus.

COMING UNLIKE HIM . . .

When Moses came to the burning bush, he discovered the presence of God in the Midian wilderness. There God told Moses, "I am who I am."[2] In this scene God makes clear that He alone is self-existent, independent of anything and anyone in the universe He has created ex nihilo. God's creation, recounted in Genesis 1, is independent of matter, because He made matter. Then, having made the clay, He uses it to shape His artwork. God is independent in a way freedom-loving people have difficulty grasping. We are, theoretically at least, free within fairly narrow limits of law, opportunity, and

> In coming to God *unlike* Him, Moses was able to receive from God the grace to be more *like* Him.

giftedness. God, however, is truly autonomous, constrained only by the free exercise of His own will.

Before Moses could know and serve this self-existent Lord, he had to understand what God is like, and what he himself was like. Now understand that Moses was not a man of illusions. He was aware of his many weaknesses. "Who am I," Moses asked God, "that I should go to Pharaoh and bring the children of Israel out of Egypt?"[3] Moses was a man in complete dependence. He came to God unlike Him—the weak before the strong. In coming to God *unlike* Him, Moses was able to receive from God the grace to be more *like* Him.It all began with honesty about his limits before the perfect, unlimited God. He came to God unlike Him that he might go into the world very much like Him.

Moses' transformation was not based on any moral striving. He met God dependent upon Him, then he went back into God's world more like God. Surely God's ringing answer to Moses' confession of weakness—"I will be with you"[4]—was a great encouragement as he did.

GOING MORE LIKE HIM

If we discover our unloveliness at the very moment we have uttered a cross word at another person, we can go to God, unlike Him in all of our unloveliness, that we might draw love from Him— the love that ever loves the undeserving and unlovely. Then, basking in God's love, we can return to the world, still full of weakness and unloveliness, and love more as He does, without condition.

When we are impatient, we go to God unlike Him, drawing on the reservoir of His patience, that we might be more patient with others. When we are unforgiving, we go to God unlike Him,

drawing on the reservoir of His forgiveness, that we might be more
forgiving with others. When we
are unkind, we go to God unlike
Him, drawing on the reservoir
of His kindness, that we might
be more kind with others.

No matter how many good deeds we do, if we do not engage others verbally, we are not presenting the gospel.

This principle is critical to
the sacramental evangelist. People
are more likely to hear the gospel
from a patient and understanding disciple of Christ than from an impatient one. As we
practice, in our weakness, going to God for His strength, others
will quickly begin to see something of the presence of God in us.
We will be mirroring Christ to a watching world.

We have died to the world and been raised with Christ.[5] As
new creations appointed to be God's ambassadors to the world,[6]
we must grasp that we are strategically placed to reach those He
loves with the message of His grace. When Jerry was a pastor, a
longtime member of the church approached him one Sunday
morning with a problem.

"Pastor, there is a man sitting in my pew," she said. "Would you
please tell him to move so I can sit down?"

Jerry's initial urge was to stick a finger in his ear to remove the
wax that must have impaired his hearing. There was no wax, of
course. This woman, marinating in her sense of entitlement, had
decided that the man who had taken her seat was nothing but an
inconvenience.

"You know," Jerry said to her, "if I were a betting man, I would
bet that this man sitting in your pew is a visitor and doesn't know

the rules here at this church. Perhaps you could let him have your pew this Sunday and sit behind him and pray for him during the service. Perhaps you could engage him in a friendly conversation after the service, and maybe invite him and his family to your house someday for dinner. Perhaps you could even ask him what brought him to the service this morning. Maybe his heart is troubled and you could introduce him to the very Christ he is looking for. Wouldn't that be fun?"

To her credit, the woman went back and sat behind the man. After the service, she talked to him with a big smile on her face and kindness in her eyes. She found joy in encouraging that man in Jesus.

What if each Sunday every Christian chose to be pastor of his or her pew? Every week people come to church looking for something to mend the brokenness they feel inside. Often they leave and no one has spoken a word to them the entire morning. Why? Our mirrors are dirty. Jesus isn't being reflected to others because we are not revealing ourselves to Him first. The world sees our lack of love rather than His love. But we can do something about that. We can go to God unlike Him that we might be more like Him in the world.

DO . . . BUT SPEAK

And to be like Him we need to study what He did. No matter how many good deeds we do, if we do not engage others verbally, we are not presenting the gospel, which, after all, is good *news*. Further, we cannot even be sure what impressions others are picking up from our nonverbal witness. We are always wise to combine words and deeds.

Jesus also spoke strategically, engaging people in conversations by asking questions, listening well, and going through open doors. As we will see in the next chapter, Jesus met people, addressing present needs in order to bring them into an awareness of their deeper spiritual needs. Some may criticize this approach to ministry as too people-centered. But perhaps it is more God-centered than we realize at first glance, for it seeks to work with situations, events, and longings that God has sovereignly placed in His world and in the human heart.

The good news must not be proclaimed only verbally, but also visually. God came to us in Christ. He took on human nature in order to communicate the gospel to others. It is an old strategy, and still a useful one.

Art historian Hans Rookmaaker once noted that Christ did not come to make us *Christian*; He came to make us *fully human.*[7] When men and women are redeemed in Christ, we receive power to achieve God's purpose to grow in holiness, which is why He created us. If we redeemed sinners are wise, we shouldn't seek to clean up our own acts; we should seek to reflect Him. So let us discover what God wants to make of us in Christ and then go back into the world, mirroring Him to others.

Discussion Questions

I. Do you know other Christians—apart from church friends— in your workplace or community? Have you ever considered praying and strategizing with them on how you might together love those in your world to Christ? What might this look like?

If there are no others in your surroundings who seem to know Christ, have you ever considered that God may have strategically placed you where you are in order to use you there?

2. We all have shortcomings. Have you discovered anything in your life lately (a bad habit, an annoying characteristic, a distracting behavior, a quick temper, impatience with others) that is very much unlike Christ? Could you confess it to God and some close friends? Could you go to God unlike Him and ask Him to give you what you need to be more like Him in the world? How could this help you be a better sacramental evangelist?

3. As Moses defined himself by who he was in relation to God in order to do God's work in his world, what would it look like if you redefined yourself for the work He has called you to do? What is your evangelistic mission and calling? Who are the people to whom God wants you to mirror His character and grace?

4. Have you ever considered becoming the pastor of the pew where you sit on Sunday morning? Have you considered praying during the week for those who will be sitting around you on the coming Sunday? How can you share the gospel with the people God brings into your church and places in close proximity to you?

5. How would a commitment to minister Christ to others transform the very words you use with them? How would it affect the life you live before a watching world? If your church did this corporately, what would this look like for your community at large? What can you do to make it happen?

PART 3

THE GOSPEL
AND HUMANITY

11. Points of Connection

12. Longing: *Pilgrim*

13. Longing: *Lover*

14. Longing: *Ascetic/Saint*

15. Other Longings

We need to learn the art of asking questions, and the closely related art of listening.

II) POINTS OF CONNECTION

Lee Strobel, the well-known Christian apologist and author, says we have reached a new day in sharing the gospel. The old, sure-fire gospel methods now often misfire. It's not that people won't listen to our outlines. Techniques, verses, and ready gospel facts certainly have their place in the quiver of the sacramental evangelist. But gone are the days when we could just whip through a basic gospel presentation and see people convinced intellectually and give their hearts to Jesus. He says we have to add a story of our encounter with the living Christ.

"That's what my ministry is about," Strobel told Stan. "I tell my story: I was an atheist. I scoffed. My wife became a Christian. It prompted me to investigate. Here's the evidence I found, how I received Christ, the difference it's made. It's a story. And I found that in postmodern America, people are often willing to engage on the level of story."[1]

If an evangelist as accomplished as Lee Strobel thinks we need to clothe our gospel facts in stories, then perhaps *we* should as well. Of course, while establishing personal points of connection with listeners may be the latest trend in witnessing, it is not really new. Jesus did it all the time. Let's take some time to savor the way He established points of connection with the woman at the well in Samaria:

> And [Jesus] had to pass through Samaria. So he came to a town of Samaria called Sychar, near the field that Jacob had given to his son Joseph. Jacob's well was there; so Jesus, wearied as he was from his journey, was sitting beside the well. It was about the sixth hour.
>
> A woman from Samaria came to draw water. Jesus said to her, "Give me a drink." (For his disciples had gone away into the city to buy food.) The Samaritan woman said to him, "How is it that you, a Jew, ask for a drink from me, a woman of Samaria?" (For Jews have no dealings with Samaritans.) Jesus answered her, "If you knew the gift of God, and who it is that is saying to you, 'Give me a drink,' you would have asked him, and he would have given you living water." The woman said to him, "Sir, you have nothing to draw water with, and the well is deep. Where do you get that living water? Are you greater than our father Jacob? He gave us the well and drank from it himself, as did his sons and his livestock." Jesus said to her, "Everyone who drinks of this water will be thirsty again, but whoever drinks of the water that I will give him will never be thirsty again. The water that I will give him will become in him a spring of water welling up to eternal life." The woman said to him, "Sir, give me this water, so that I will not be thirsty or have to come here to draw water."
>
> Jesus said to her, "Go, call your husband, and come here."

The woman answered him, "I have no husband." Jesus said to her, "You are right in saying, 'I have no husband'; for you have had five husbands, and the one you now have is not your husband. What you have said is true." The woman said to him, "Sir, I perceive that you are a prophet. Our fathers worshiped on this mountain, but you say that in Jerusalem is the place where people ought to worship." Jesus said to her, "Woman, believe me, the hour is coming when neither on this mountain nor in Jerusalem will you worship the Father. You worship what you do not know; we worship what we know, for salvation is from the Jews. But the hour is coming, and is now here, when the true worshipers will worship the Father in spirit and truth, for the Father is seeking such people to worship him. God is spirit, and those who worship him must worship in spirit and truth." The woman said to him, "I know that Messiah is coming (he who is called Christ). When he comes, he will tell us all things." Jesus said to her, "I who speak to you am he."

Just then his disciples came back. They marveled that he was talking with a woman, but no one said, "What do you seek?" or, "Why are you talking with her?" So the woman left her water jar and went away into town and said to the people, "Come, see a man who told me all that I ever did. Can this be the Christ?" They went out of the town and were coming to him.

. . . Many Samaritans from that town believed in him because of the woman's testimony, "He told me all that I ever did." So when the Samaritans came to him, they asked him to stay with them, and he stayed there two days. And many more believed because of his word. They said to the woman,

"It is no longer because of what you said that we believe, for we have heard for ourselves, and we know that this is indeed the Savior of the world."[2]

Note that Jesus used what was ready at hand to bring into the light a deeper spiritual need. With the woman at the well, the initial point of connection was water. They were both thirsty, and Jesus asked her for a drink. In asking for water, of course, Jesus stepped outside of cultural conventions. He was a Jewish man, she a Samaritan woman. But the connection was made, and it awakened in her a curiosity that led to deeper heart issues and, in short order, her salvation, and the salvation of many of her neighbors.

BUILDING RELATIONSHIPS

Certainly on the surface it seems to be more difficult to build relationships than it used to be.

Baron Friedrich von Hugel, an Austrian nobleman and Christian apologist at the turn of the twentieth century, understood well the need to meet people where they are in order to take them where they need to be. "I want to make the most of whatever light people have got, however slight it may be," von Hugel said, "to strengthen and deepen whatever they already possess if I can."[3] We use the word "make" advisedly, since our sacramental understanding of God means that He is already present in the life of the other person, before we ever open our mouths.

And since God is with this person, we can trust that we will discover mutual points of connection. We need to connect with people at any given moment and in any setting. So pray for God to open your eyes and give you the insight and words you need as you speak with others.

Certainly on the surface it seems to be more difficult to build relationships than it used to be. Modern society has brought many blessings: vaccinations, appliances, technology, mobility, and so on. But our very mobility as a society erodes traditional social ties and encourages both anonymity and distrust of strangers. We can connect through the Internet with people across the world but somehow have little to say to our next-door neighbors.

In 2006, the *American Sociological Review* published a study that should give us pause, "Social Isolation in America." Researchers Miller McPherson, Lynn Smith-Lovin, and Matthew E. Brashears reported a "remarkable drop" in the number of people who were able to discuss important matters with others.

The study found that, as of 2004, the average American had just two close friends, compared with an average of three in 1985. Those reporting none multiplied from 10 percent to 25 percent. The share of Americans reporting as many as four or five friends, meanwhile, plunged from 33 percent to just over 15 percent.[4]

In other words, the sacramental evangelist will have to work harder than ever before to build trust and establish relationships with others. But don't worry; if you listen to the God who walks alongside, your efforts will be rewarded. You will stand out from our darkening culture like a "star in the universe."[5] People will see you as someone who is interested in them and is approachable. This is not rocket science. Decades ago, Dale Carnegie, author of the bestselling *How to Win Friends and Influence People*, pointed out that those who are genuinely interested in others often gain a hearing for themselves.[6]

HAVING SOMETHING TO TALK ABOUT

We will need, of course, a growing understanding of the nature of life. We cannot effectively talk with others if we do not have something worth saying. As we have said, Bible verses, as good and important as they are in themselves, are usually not enough to generate a desire to understand the gospel or lead someone to Jesus. We need to know how to connect, and having a variety of interests to talk about will help us do so. While we shouldn't wait to share our faith with others, neither should we shrink from doing the hard work to get better at it.

While the secrets of the kingdom are not revealed to the self-proclaimed wise,[7] ignorance for the sake of ignorance is no virtue. We are responsible to take whatever talents the Lord has given us and multiply them for greater effectiveness in the kingdom.[8]

For example, a good liberal arts education generally will help us to see and connect more widely with different kinds of people. Note the mission statement of Wheaton College, where Jerry teaches: "Wheaton College exists to help build the church and improve society worldwide by promoting the development of whole and effective Christians through excellence in programs of Christian higher education. This mission expresses our commitment to do all things—'for Christ and His Kingdom.'" The liberal arts, grounded in a solidly biblical worldview, should lead us to good reading, self-awareness, and social, psychological, and emotional connectedness. These qualities should open us up to people and their complexities.

If a liberal arts education is not possible, we should stay as informed and engaged in the broader culture as possible. We also need to read widely—not only current bestsellers but also the classics (see chapter 12 for a discussion of the classics).

Then we need to learn the art of asking questions, and the closely related art of listening (in a way that reveals genuine interest in others). Follow the example of Jesus, who was an unparalleled questioner and listener.[9] Doing so will open doors for the gospel.

Here's a basic rule of thumb: *Go as deep as the person you are speaking with will allow.* Begin with public topics common to you both. Then move into other, deeper areas the person leaves open to you through his or her answers.

Note what Jesus does with a certain inquirer named Nicodemus:

The sacramental evangelist will study Jesus' encounters with the spiritually needy and be alert for contemporary applications.

Now there was a man of the Pharisees named Nicodemus, a ruler of the Jews. This man came to Jesus by night and said to him, "Rabbi, we know that you are a teacher come from God, for no one can do these signs that you do unless God is with him." Jesus answered him, "Truly, truly, I say to you, unless one is born again he cannot see the kingdom of God." Nicodemus said to him, "How can a man be born when he is old? Can he enter a second time into his mother's womb and be born?" Jesus answered, "Truly, truly, I say to you, unless one is born of water and the Spirit, he cannot enter the kingdom of God. That which is born of the flesh is flesh, and that which is born of the Spirit is spirit. Do not marvel that I said to you, 'You must be born again.' The wind blows where it wishes, and you hear its sound, but you do not know where it comes from or where it goes. So it is with everyone who is born of the Spirit."[10]

Nicodemus asks a theological question. Jesus answers him using the metaphor of birth. He does this because some things can only be explained by way of analogy. According to Merriam-Webster's, an analogy is a "resemblance in some particulars between things otherwise unlike."[11] Jesus uses something He and Nicodemus have in common—physical birth—to move to the deeper topic of spiritual birth.

With the sick man at the Pool of Bethesda,[12] Jesus worked with the local belief that people could be healed if they reached the water first. The Gospels are full of these encounters between Jesus and the spiritually needy. The sacramental evangelist will study them and be alert for contemporary applications.

MOVIES, MUSIC, AND MORE

What raw material can we use to strike up a conversation? Books and movies play a profound role in Western culture and provide many avenues to fruitful explorations of issues. Note the general progression in the following questions from public issues into deeper topics:

- How do the characters handle key life issues—work, family, alienation, and so on?

- How do the characters respond to situations and plot turns?
- Which character did you most identify with and why?
- What did you find most admirable in the character you identified with?
- Which character did you find most irritating and why?
- What were the unmet needs of the character you found irritating?
- What did that character want?
- What was he or she trying to accomplish?
- Was the character going about it in a good way or a bad way?
- How do you make judgments as to what is good or bad, right or wrong?
- Were the needs of the various characters good or bad?
- Did the characters act fairly?
- Was their attempt to fulfill their needs fair? Why do you think so?
- What do you think Jesus would do for this person if He were to meet those needs in a loving way?

If no books or movies are at hand, talk about something else that interests you or the other person. At Starbucks or Caribou you can discuss coffee—how it is grown, the economics of coffee, fair trade and social justice issues, the dignity of humanity, and so on.

At the park you can discuss the weather, the dog being walked, or some other topic that lends itself naturally to mentioning God's creative greatness. On an airplane you can discuss travel and the pilgrim longing (see the next chapter), or perhaps the fear of travel. At a funeral you can naturally talk about death, missing loved ones, practical concerns, and other topics. You can comment on commonly shared and noted current events. When listening to music, remark about how amazing it is that we can enjoy it and mention that you think it is a gift from God. Ask where a person is from and prepare to go deeper. He or she may mention a divorce or speak wistfully of some long gone place.

As you broach these topics, think about generic—unthreatening—follow-up questions. Good questions awaken curiosity and focus attention on unmet needs only Jesus has the capacity to fulfill. The aim is to go as deep as your companion will allow.

"Our Lord tells us not to put out the smoking flax, not to break the bruised reed—and yet I always see *this*," Baron von Hugel said. "God makes lovely little flowers to grow everywhere, but someone always comes and sits on them."[13]

FACING PAINFUL TOPICS

Relationships often bring our deepest joys . . . and our deepest sorrows. Being honestly in touch with your own relational successes and struggles may help you open up the conversation further. Be careful not to talk too much about yourself, however. Use your experience as a gentle transition for the *other* person to open up. Here are some innocuous queries: Do you have siblings? Are you married? Do you have children? Then listen.

> **B**ecause we are made in God's image, our only lasting satisfaction must be found in Him.

Validate pain, anger, disappointment, bitterness, and struggle. They are all around us, and for good reason, whether experienced personally or collectively as a family or even a nation. Our pain, when not given to God, produces bitterness that kills. "In fact," Anne Lamott has written, "not forgiving is like drinking rat poison and waiting for the rat to die."[14]

Do not shy away from such expressions of pain. They may seem like barriers to faith but in fact simply could be the rubble of human brokenness. When this rubble is cleared away, a person's heart may open, allowing him or her to believe the gospel.

Because we are made in God's image, our only lasting satisfaction must be found in Him. But too few people realize this truth. "There is one elementary fact which is quite obvious," Albert Schweitzer said. "The disastrous feature of our civilization is that it is far more developed materially than spiritually."[15] And remember, Schweitzer wrote this in 1922—long before the Internet, DVDs, iPods, iPads, and whatever other electronic devices come our way!

So watch for deeper points of connection with your fellow image-bearers. Since God is present, they will be there. Just remember, one person's search for God may well look different than another's. Jesus is the only way to God, but the way to Jesus is unique for each of us.

Discussion Questions

I. What factors cause conversations to get under way with people you've just met? How did relationships with your close friends develop? What can you draw on in your own experience that might help you cultivate relationships with others to win their trust and tell them about Christ?

2. A point of connection with a fellow human being begins by asking public questions about things commonly shared. What are some common things you can ask about on a first meeting that might initiate a conversation? How might you draw out the perspective of others into meaningful and non-judgmental conversation in order to get to know that person and become aware of God's individual work in his or her life?

3. There is an art to asking questions and listening interactively. Have you ever considered that this art might develop as you cultivate a sense of curiosity, wonder, and awe? What are you doing to cultivate these things now? How can you develop a growing interest in the unique people all around you, each of whom was made by God and in whom He delights? How might this curiosity and wonder make you a better evangelist?

4. What books have you read recently? What movies have you seen? What current events have occurred that could occasion a conversation about spiritual things? Explain how you might use the book, the film, or the current event to open a conversation to a discussion of deeper matters.

5. Is our world more developed materially than spiritually? Explain why you think so. Could it be that people are still spiritually inclined and interested even though fewer may be talking about deep things in public settings? Pray that God grants you the grace to segue conversations naturally into the regions where people are so hungry and yet many are unwilling to bring these things up. What might this look like in your sphere of influence?

Many lesser things threaten to divert us from our true destination, and our heart can become blind and deaf to the "better country."

12) LONGING: *PILGRIM*

Evelyn Underhill, the first woman given university-wide lecture status at Oxford, identified three deep human cravings. She called them the "three great expressions of man's restlessness, which only mystic truth can fully satisfy. The first is the craving which makes him a pilgrim and wanderer. It is the longing to go out from his normal world in search of a lost home, a 'better country'; an Eldorado, a Sarras, a Heavenly Syon."[1] (We will examine Underhill's other two longings in subsequent chapters.)

The word *pilgrim* often conjures up an image of brown-clad travelers on their way to the New World and the first Thanksgiving. *Pilgrimage* sounds ancient, even archaic, to postmodern ears. If we use it at all, it is in distinctly unreligious contexts: We make our pilgrimage to Wrigley Field to watch the Cubs, for example.

But however strange this concept may seem, it is deeply rooted in our religious impulse. Catholic pilgrims strain to see the pope standing on his balcony at St. Peter's Square. Others regularly make pilgrimages to places where forebears have had visions. Stan remembers visiting the ancient Polish city of Krakow before the fall of communism. Under the watchful eye of the followers of Karl Marx, a procession of pilgrims displaying Solidarity banners peacefully walked through the ancient city streets. They were headed to Czestochowa to venerate the Black Madonna, an ancient relic. Muslims, too, understand our common pilgrim longing. They are obligated to go on the *hajj* to Mecca at least once in their lifetimes, and most do so gladly.

THIS LONGING IN THE CLASSICS

The classics tap this longing—perhaps that is *why* they are classics. Homer's *Odyssey* chronicles a hero's relentless quest to return to his wife after the Trojan War. The adventures and trials of Odysseus are many, but at the center of his heart is the longing to go home. And yet when Odysseus finally arrives, he finds even more wrongs that must be righted, and that what we love best in this world can fail to satisfy.

Earthly homes may awaken this longing, but they cannot satisfy it.

Virgil tells of Aeneas, the citizen of Troy who flees the city after it has been sacked by the Greeks. His beloved wife is dead and his city is in flames. The spirit of his fallen prince, Hector, tells Aeneas that he is destined to build a new city. His wife's ghost confirms the prophecy. Aeneas's subsequent adventures are lived between two cities: Troy, the city of his birth and all his nostalgic longing; and Rome, the city that will be, the city of Aeneas's future, the city of hope.

Virgil's great *Aeneid* became a metaphor for early Christians, who recognized that they too were living between two cities. It is the same with all of us. We feel the tug of home, awakened in us by our birthplace or the places that shaped our earliest memories. On the other hand, we long for a place that will eventually satisfy our deepest aspirations and widest hopes in a way home never could. Everyone who has ever lived has been caught between the world of our birth and the world to come. God speaks to us strangers and exiles between these two worlds.

J. R. R. Tolkien, a man weaned on the classics, speaks to this longing for a place in *The Hobbit*. The book begins with a small, manlike creature named Bilbo Baggins. Bilbo is perfectly at home in his Shire. He lives in a hobbit hole in the side of a hill, "and that means comfort."[2] His comfortable life is interrupted when a wizard named Gandalf drops in to tell him that he has been selected to be the fourteenth member of a party of dwarves, whose quest is to recapture their ancient home from an evil dragon named Smaug.

The first time Bilbo has to sleep on the hard ground rather than in the soft, feathery bed of his hobbit hole, he longs for home. When his provisions grow stale, he longs for his larder. When he faces danger from trolls, Bilbo longs for the seeming security of the Shire.

Eventually the adventures end, and Bilbo can go home. It is here that Tolkien works his greatest magic. When Bilbo returns, he discovers the Shire is no longer the place of his deepest longing. His relatives have declared him dead and are dividing up his belongings. When Bilbo tries to stop them, some declare him an imposter and refuse to return what they have taken. Tolkien is being very deliberate in seeking to awaken a longing for home. He shows that what we really want is transcendent. Earthly homes may awaken this longing, but they cannot satisfy it.

LONGING FOR WHAT NEVER ENDS

Isn't this the story of every man and woman? Have you ever returned home for a class reunion? You go back to familiar places, only to discover that what you were longing for has changed. The vacant lots where you used to play baseball now have buildings on them. Familiar landmarks have been torn down to make way for new structures that don't seem to fit, at least not in your memory, and therefore either they or you are out of place. You visit the old elementary school playground. It seemed to stretch the width of a degree of longitude when you were young. Now it seems so cramped that you wonder how you ever managed.

At the reunion, you discover that the others who have come look strangely weathered. Fortunately the name tags have old yearbook photos affixed. The men are variously bald, fat, wrinkled, or sporting fringes of gray. The women are mostly unrecognizable. Clearly, life has been hard on the lot of them. You, of course, look great!

> "Maybe what you are truly longing for the most is the one thing that never has to end."

During Jerry's first stint at Wheaton College, his son Jeremy was allowed to audition for the child's role whenever a college production called for it. One day Jeremy was cast as Young Pip in the theatrical production of Charles Dickens's *Great Expectations*. For the first third of the play, he was the main character, with most of the lines. Jeremy, ten, loved the opportunity to live the life of a college thespian. He developed close friendships with his college buddies over the months of rehearsals and was thrilled by the performances.

The last night of the play, after the final performance, Jeremy came out of the dressing room wearing his street clothes. As Jerry and his son passed through the theater on the way to the parking lot, Jeremy saw something that gave him pause. The students who had worked so hard on the play were now dismantling the set. The world he had come to love was being destroyed right before his eyes. "Dad," he said weakly, "I've got to sit down."

After watching the destruction for ten or fifteen minutes, Jerry finally told his son that it was time to go. Jeremy shuffled out to the car like an old man. "Dad," he said plaintively, "I just didn't want it to end!" Expressing empathy, Jerry responded to his son, "It is the nature of every play to eventually come to an end, just like every holiday or vacation must come to an end. It's even the nature of every year of school to come to an end. In fact, it is the nature of your childhood that it will come to an end. Maybe what you are truly longing for the most is the one thing that never has to end."

He looked up. "Do you mean heaven, Dad?"

"Yes, heaven. Maybe what you really long for most is heaven."

"HOMESICK IN OUR HOMES"

The apostle Peter addressed his first epistle to pilgrims and strangers.[3] All of us are merely passing through this life. Our experience here is transient and temporary. We need something solid, something permanent. Abraham went out from Ur of the

Chaldeans because he was looking for the City with foundations, whose architect and builder is God.

> By faith Abraham obeyed when he was called to go out to a place that he was to receive as an inheritance. And he went out, not knowing where he was going. By faith he went to live in the land of promise, as in a foreign land, living in tents with Isaac and Jacob, heirs with him of the same promise. For he was looking forward to the city that has foundations, whose designer and builder is God. By faith Sarah herself received power to conceive, even when she was past the age, since she considered him faithful who had promised. Therefore from one man, and him as good as dead, were born descendants as many as the stars of heaven and as many as the innumerable grains of sand by the seashore.
>
> These all died in faith, not having received the things promised, but having seen them and greeted them from afar, and having acknowledged that they were strangers and exiles on the earth. For people who speak thus make it clear that they are seeking a homeland. If they had been thinking of that land from which they had gone out, they would have had opportunity to return. But as it is, they desire a better country, that is, a heavenly one. Therefore God is not ashamed to be called their God, for he has prepared for them a city.[4]

G. K. Chesterton once observed that people are "homesick in their homes."[5] He knew that every time we lay our heads on our pillows at the end of the day, we lay them down in a foreign land. Much of society's current concern for the environment—something good in itself—comes from the widespread belief that the "pale, blue dot" on which we find ourselves in the universe's infinite blackness is our only home.[6] But our hearts, when they are honest, tell us that our true home is to be found elsewhere.

The realization that we are strangers in this world may itself be evidence of the presence of the Spirit of God wooing us to Himself. "You stir us so that praising you may bring us joy," Augustine said, "because you have made us and drawn us to yourself, and our heart is unquiet until it rests in you."[7] Those of us practicing the sacrament of evangelism will do well to speak explicitly to this longing whenever we notice its presence in others.

THE PASSING OF TIME

Think about how often you have been surprised at the passing of time. When we were young, our ears regularly heard older people express shock at how quickly we were growing. *We* never noticed it, really. Time for us seemed to pass so slowly. When we were five, the time from one Christmas to the next took a fifth of our lives. Now, with more life behind us, each Christmas seems to come more quickly than the last. Now we are the ones who express dismay at the swift passage of time.

> The sacramental evangelist wants to touch the hearts of people who long for they know not what.

C. S. Lewis once observed that the very part of us that is surprised by time's passage speaks volumes.[8] If we are merely creatures of time, why are we so surprised? Could this paradox not be a clue itself that we are more than temporal creatures? If this is the case, how foolish it would be to live as if this life is all that matters. When our intuition seems to shout at us in this way, we would do well to listen. God speaks in and through these phenomena. A sacramental evangelist does well to work with these deep human longings. They may be evidence that God is already at work.

In *The Pilgrim's Regress*, Lewis provides an allegory whose central character, John, catches a glimpse of a faraway island. For the rest of the book he goes on a mission to find that island, to satisfy his longing. Many imposters come along and attempt to quench his spiritual thirst, but only the island—the real thing—will do. In *The Pilgrim's Regress* Lewis develops longings similar to those of Underhill and links them with periods of literature. It is fascinating and helpful reading for the sacramental evangelist who wants to touch the hearts of people who long for they know not what. But the salient point for us right now is to recognize that God speaks to people not just in their rationality but in the deep longings of their hearts.

For Lewis, the subject was far from academic. *The Pilgrim's Regress* contains a large helping of autobiography. "From childhood," J. I. Packer and Jerry write, "Lewis had known moments of what he called *joy*; meaning, very precisely, a sweet ache of sensing—and in that moment longing for—a reality of life, light, and beauty beyond ordinary experience. These aching moments, which he thought were common (though constantly misperceived), set a person searching for something not yet known."[9]

We all have an island toward which we are drawn. Many lesser things threaten to divert us—money, sex, success, an easy life—from our true destination, and our heart can become blind and deaf to the "better country." But the sacramental evangelist knows that these longings provide openings to people's souls, that ultimately our hearts are restless without God. So there is no need to force the issue—God is already calling.

Discussion Questions

1. Do you ever feel the tug of nostalgic longing for some place? Describe it. Have you ever felt that this kind of longing could be common and could also provide an opening for the gospel?

2. As the world undergoes constant change, do you ever long for something more permanent? What might that tell you about your nature? Could it be that God has built into us the anticipation for both permanence and constant change? How may this fact affect how you do evangelism? How might God meet you in these places of your life; and in these places in the lives of those you share with?

3. What did G. K. Chesterton mean when he said, "We are homesick in our own homes"? How does this longing connect with a transcendent longing for heaven?

4. Has some event or experience awakened in you a longing for a place that transcends the best temporal expressions of home? Have you ever felt homesick only to discover on arriving home that you were longing for something more? Do you think that as you develop your own sensitivities to this kind of longing that you may become better equipped to speak more freely about this kind of longing with others?

5. Describe how God might be wooing others to Himself through this pilgrim longing. How could you bring this up in a conversation with others? What kinds of events or experiences might serve as bridges to connect the gospel to this deep longing?

Those who have found the love of Christ and who want to tell others about it will do well to work with their awakening sense that Someone is missing.

13) LONGING: *LOVER*

Jerry first heard about the great Italian poet Dante Alighieri in seventh grade. He can still picture the yellow textbook with a drawing of Dante at the Ponte Vecchio in Florence as Beatrice Portinari walks by. But what really sticks in his mind is what his teacher said: "Dante, while just a boy of nine, noticed a girl of his city, named Beatrice. He saw her only a handful of times in his life. He lit a candle of devotion to her in his heart. Though he married someone else and raised his children by this other woman, he left his heart's devotion aflame for Beatrice."

Jerry decided that Dante was not a nice man.

Many years later, after Jerry's conversion to Christ, he became fascinated by the writings of C. S. Lewis and the constellation of authors associated with him, including Charles Williams and Dorothy Sayers. As he voraciously read their works, he began to uncomfortably notice that they all loved Dante. Lewis thought he was the greatest poet. Williams wrote *The Figure of Beatrice*. Sayers learned Italian and produced the first English translation of *The Divine Comedy* that maintained the original rhyming.

Faced with a dilemma, Jerry decided to lay aside his prejudices and pick up Dante afresh. In Dante's first book, *Vita Nuova*, or *New Life*, the poet, who was in his early twenties, chronicles how he met Beatrice and wonders what it is she means to him. The impression she made was unforgettable.

> I felt a sleeping spirit in my heart
> Awake to Love, and then from far away
> I saw the Lord of Love approaching me,
> and hardly recognized him through joy.
> "Think now of nothing but to honor me,"
> I heard him say each word with a smile.[1]

In a world made by God, many things possess the potential to awaken in us a longing for Him. For Dante it could have been a sunrise or a sunset, the stars in the night sky, the droplets decorating a rose on a summer's morning, a cooing dove in an elm tree on a lazy afternoon. But in the providence of God, it was a young woman named Beatrice.

Some twenty-five years later, Dante wrote *The Divine Comedy* with its three installments: the *Inferno*, *Purgatorio*, and *Paradiso*. At the beginning Dante discovers himself to be on the threshold of hell and receives a guide to lead him on a journey: Virgil, another poet of longing. Halfway through the *Purgatorio*, Beatrice, who has died, descends from

> Sacramental evangelists have the privilege of speaking explicitly to others at their place of deep relational longing.

heaven and guides him onward. She eventually deposits Dante at the threshold of the vision of God, leaving the poet to press on into the archetypal and primary relationship, which is found in the presence of God. Dante makes it clear that the longing awakened by earthly loves ultimately can only be filled by God.

Lover is Evelyn Underhill's second longing. The sacramental evangelist knows that God draws people through this longing, because only He can satisfy it.

SHORTCOMINGS OF RELATIONSHIPS

Thirst indicates that you need a drink, hunger a need for food. Loneliness says you long for relationship. But have you ever felt lonely in a crowd or when living under the same roof with others who love and care for you? Perhaps this unexpected loneliness doesn't prove anything, but it does suggest that you were made for something no mere human relationship can satisfy. While other relationships are very important, the one we long for most deeply is a relationship with God. God speaks implicitly to all of us in this way. Sacramental evangelists have the privilege of speaking explicitly to others at their place of deep relational longing.

- Human relationships can be fulfilling, but they cannot ultimately fulfill.
- Marriage is fulfilling, but it doesn't perfectly satisfy.
- Having children is fulfilling, but children do not end this longing.
- Having a career you enjoy may be fulfilling, but it cannot bring peace.

If we expect our spouses to fulfill us, it won't be long before we will be disappointed and will project that disappointment onto them. Our spouses did nothing wrong; it is our misplaced expectation that leads to crushing disappointment. When the sacramental evangelist discovers this disappointment in others, he or she needs to work with it in order to point them to Christ. Remember, God can be found in the emptiness. So listen to people's stories and become aware of the places where God is already speaking into their hearts.

Many people, of course, don't recognize God's voice and so attempt to fulfill their longings in sinful ways. Henry Guthrie, the earliest known ancestor on Stan's father's side, was born somewhere in Georgia around the year 1812. A record of Henry's 1834 marriage to Manerva Lyons exists at the Newton County Courthouse in Covington. The census of 1840 shows Henry and Manerva still living in Newton County, with one child and two other adults (probably relatives).

Over the next ten years, the Guthries moved to Cobb County, where Henry was a shoemaker, as well as a farmer. He and Manerva had seven other children, one of whom died. It was likely a hard life, as the mid-nineteenth century was for many. Family stories say that sometime before 1860, Henry Guthrie left his family to join a gold rush, possibly in northern Georgia. He was never heard from again.[2]

CYCLES OF DISAPPOINTMENT

Whatever happened to break up the family, it is an old story. We forsake our sacred commitments in a futile attempt to find something better elsewhere. When Lewis was on his pilgrimage

to faith, he observed that he was practicing what he called a kind of
"dialectic of desire."[3] Borrowing
from Georg Wilhelm Friedrich
Hegel, who believed that history moves with a kind of
dialectic of thesis, antithesis, and
synthesis, Lewis used this
approach (which he called a
myth) as an analogy to describe the
universal quest for something, or
someone. Lewis said his interest would be
awakened by a particular object. This would lead to a soaring
expectation that what aroused his interest had the capacity to fulfill his deepest desires.

> **G**od is present in the awakening of desire. He uses the things of this world to woo us to Himself.

Over time, however, Lewis realized that what had awakened
his desire was impotent to actually fulfill that desire. So Lewis's
hopes and expectations came crashing into disappointments until
something else caught his attention. Again, his expectations soared
with this newly desired object—until its incapacity to satisfy him
became manifest.

Lewis found himself going through repeated cycles of tethering his heart to objects of expectation, falling into disappointment, untethering his heart, and seeking some other object. This
was the dialectic of desire. Lewis eventually realized that what he
was ultimately looking for could not be found in any mutable
object. Lewis was longing for something immutable and unchang-
ing. He was searching for eternity. He was looking for God.

LASTING ENJOYMENT

There is something of the sacramental in this quest. God is present in the awakening of desire. He uses the things of this world to woo us to Himself. He is a relational God who longs for each of us to be satisfied relationally in Him first and foremost if we are to find positive enjoyment in other relationships. God awakens desire through the things He has made. God also, in His mercy, allows for the disappointments when we tether those desires to objects that cannot fulfill. God guides the process because He wants us to discover our greatest fulfillment in His unconditional love and complete forgiveness.

The dialectic of desire, followed properly through all of its ups and downs, eventually leads people to the One object of desire who can truly fulfill. *The sacramental evangelist does well to work with what God is already doing in people's lives.* When we do, we can gently nudge seeking souls toward the One who is already present and who loves them the most.

Ecclesiastes displays a gritty realism about the human condition. Note the flow of its argument, because it can help you connect the gospel to those who have sought God in all the wrong places.

> We live in a world in which we long to find joy and happiness. But these can only be found if we begin with God.

- 1:1–2: All is vanity without God.
- 2:25: Only God provides lasting enjoyment.

- 3:11: God has put a longing for eternity in our hearts.
- 12:13: Put God first in your life.

Some have called the poetic books of the Bible the "how-to" books of Scripture. Job is about how to suffer and make sense of it. The book of Psalms is about how to praise God in the good times and in the bad. Proverbs is about how to make good decisions and grow in practical ways. The Song of Solomon is about how to cultivate a relationship that produces fruit. Ecclesiastes, however, leaves readers scratching their heads. What is Ecclesiastes about? *It simply teaches us how to enjoy life.*

FALLING INTO PLACE

Ecclesiastes begins with the observation, "I have seen everything that is done under the sun, and behold, all is vanity and a striving after wind."[4] "Under the sun" is the operative phrase throughout the book. None of life makes sense if we only have an "under the sun" perspective. Nothing under the sun can ultimately satisfy because we were made to find our satisfaction in God.

Of course, we live in a world in which we long to find joy and happiness. But Ecclesiastes says these can only be found if we begin with God. The key verse is 2:25: "for apart from him who can eat or who can have enjoyment?" Take God out of the equation and life doesn't make sense. Put God first and things start to fall into place. Give me the world without God and I will still feel the gnawing emptiness. Life without God will not ultimately satisfy. As Jesus asked, "For what does it profit a man to gain the whole world and forfeit his soul?"[5] But give me God and I will find joy amid the things of this world.

SECURE IN GOD'S LOVE

Many people you meet today are disappointed in love. Failed relationships have left their hearts broken, even bitter. While breakups are a common part of life, the pain they can cause may be a symptom of something deeper. It could be that the disappointment signifies that the brokenhearted are looking for a kind of love no mere mortal could ever give. But secure in God's love, I will be able to appreciate relationships and material things for what they can give, and I will stop expecting to gain from them what they cannot give. On days when the world seems to be unraveling, my heart will be steady because it is fixed on the only one who can bring ultimate satisfaction. I will hold firm because my life is built not on sand but on the rock.[6]

> **C**hange came as they experienced an emerging sense of God as the great and unconditional Lover of their souls.

The ancients called this approach *ordo amoris*, or ordered love. They also called it a hierarchy of love. *Hierarchy* comes from two Greek words: *hieron*, meaning temple or holy place, and *archon*, meaning rule; thus hierarchy means "holy rule." The Bible teaches that we humans do best when we cultivate a "holy rule" of love. This hierarchy means we are to love God first and foremost, finding our ultimate satisfaction in Him. Then we can enter human relationships and all they can give without false or unrealistic expectations.

Jerry once met a man who was deeply disappointed. His expectations of his wife were so high that they imperiled their marriage.

Frustrated that she could not do what only God could do, during an argument he struck her, and she filed for divorce. The wife had her own expectations, which also came crashing down around her.

Neither of them actually wanted a divorce. Both simply wanted to be loved unconditionally, but neither had the capacity to do this. Jerry listened to both their stories and experienced the joy of leading them to Christ, the great Lover of their souls. When the husband and wife found Christ and centered their lives in the security of His love for them, they discovered resources to rekindle their love for each other at a more honest, realistic level. This change required a lot of humility and grace and did not happen overnight. But in time the change came as they experienced an emerging sense of God as the great and unconditional Lover of their souls. Going to God unlike Him, they were able to begin acting like Him, albeit imperfectly, toward each other.

Seeing God in this way allows us to avoid the idolatry that puts others in God's place. We can then give love with a greater sense of security. We will never love others perfectly, nor will they love us perfectly. Only God can do that. If others expect us to provide the perfect love that only God can give, we will become anxious. But if other people in our life are cultivating satisfaction in God, they will be able to appreciate the imperfect love we can give because their ultimate security rests in Christ.

The sacramental evangelist can connect people with the true Source of their longings. Those who have found the love of Christ and who want to tell others about it will do well to work with their awakening sense that something—or, better—Someone is missing. There is joy in introducing others to the One who loves them most.

Once a man came to Jerry's church looking for answers. His

girlfriend had ended their relationship that week, and he was devastated. As Jerry and the visitor sat together in the pew after the service, Jerry couldn't help but wonder if God was speaking to the man's heart through his unfulfilled longings.

After listening to the man's story, Jerry told him about the banquet of God's love for him, a love that would not let him go. The man's hungry heart opened wide to receive what God was offering him that moment in Christ. This man, of course, still had some grieving to do over the loss of his girlfriend, but God would be with him in the mending process, and he knew it. Jerry was privileged over the next several years to watch the man fall deeply in love with God, eventually marry someone else, and go into a ministry in which he has been able to speak of the love of God to others whose hearts had also been broken with lover longing.

Out of his pain the man reordered his love and became a sacramental evangelist. So can you.

Discussion Questions

I. Have you ever had a Beatrician experience such as Dante had? Describe it.

2. Do you think these relational awakenings are common? Why do you think this might (or might not) be so? Is it possible that someone, or some experience, could trigger in you a longing for a Lover who has loved you for all eternity?

3. Have you ever tethered your heart to a mutable object, only to be disappointed when you discovered that the object could not permanently fulfill? What happened? How could this experience be useful in presenting the gospel to others?

4. Earthly relationships can bring great satisfaction and fulfillment. What kind of joy have you found in relationships? While joy certainly can be found in connection with others, is it relevant to speak of a primary relationship with God that makes sense of all other relationships? Why, or why not?

5. Are you willing to share your own story of discovering God's deep love for you? Share that story with someone and see if that fellow seeker connects with the circumstances you describe.

Whenever you meet someone who has come to understand his or her brokenness and desires to be mended, you can safely assume that God is present and at work.

14) LONGING:
ASCETIC/SAINT

Years ago Jerry was talking with a seminary president who estimated that 60 percent of the students graduating and going into ministry were wounded people. Jerry looked him in the eye and replied, "I think it is 100 percent of us who are wounded." Smiling with grim agreement, the president admitted the truth of the observation.

Discussing the encounter later, however, a theologian friend asked Jerry to clarify what he meant by *wounded*. If Jerry meant *fallen*, then of course all human beings are indeed wounded, for all of us are both sinful and flawed.[1] But he went on to say that if by *wounded*, Jerry meant *broken*—that is, *aware* that we are wounded—then not all are.

This is an important distinction. Sometimes we throw around the word *wounded* so breezily that we excuse ourselves from personal responsibility. It is easy to become so familiar with our woundedness, and so practiced in making excuses for our sins, shortcomings, and failures, that we become blind to our need for forgiveness and grace. We stop striving for holiness. We are *wounded*, after all, and so can't be expected to do any better.

But sometimes we encounter people whose eyes have been opened to their fallenness and who want to do something about it. They are not only aware of their brokenness; they are on a quest to find mending. This is Evelyn Underhill's third primal drive of the human race—the *ascetic* and *saint* longing.

BROKENNESS AND GOD'S WORK

Whenever you meet someone who has come to understand his or her brokenness and desires to be mended, you can safely assume that God is present and at work. The sacrament of evangelism is apparent as God woos people to Himself through their honest assessment of deep need.

It has always been this way. When the Christian church was still in its infancy, many people went into the desert to live as hermits. The Desert Fathers would retreat to seek God and mend, engaging in lives of contemplation, weeping over their sin, and praying for grace and understanding.

When we keep in mind our own brokenness, the risk of arrogance and condescension is reduced.

While, sadly, we have some accounts from this era of abusive religious practice, we also possess elevated stories of men and women whose honesty about their personal failure and sin led them to discover depths of God's grace. Many became sought-after spiritual guides for those who needed help with their own deep wounds, sorrows, and failures. From this period of history, Underhill recognized a kind of longing that desperately wants the broken pieces of life put back together.

The point isn't that we need to find the flaws of others. Instead, we gently work with people who already know they are flawed. The sacramental evangelist must constantly remember his or her *own* brokenness. This memory reminds us that our need for Christ is not casual; it is constant. When we keep in mind our own brokenness, the risk of arrogance and condescension is reduced. We will be less likely to talk down to others. We will speak to everyone we meet as pilgrims on the same road, seeking to discover ever-deepening applications of the grace of God in our lives. An awareness of God's grace at the place of our own brokenness allows us to approach others with vulnerability and honesty that invite open responses.

PRIME RIB AND PERFECTION

Jerry was once invited to preach during Evensong at one of the Oxford University colleges. Following the service, he was privileged to eat at the high table. High table at an Oxford college is memorable, to say the least. (The *Harry Potter* films provide a glimpse—the dining hall at Hogwarts is actually taken from the Great Hall at Christ Church College at Oxford.)

Jerry was to enjoy his meal in a cavernous space with high, honey-colored walls and dark wood paneling. Imposing paintings of benefactors and famous graduates peered down on those assembled, as if reminding them that this was an august place full of privilege—not that anyone needed to be reminded.

Long tables where the students dine run the length of the hall. At one end, perpendicular to the student tables and elevated about three steps, is the high table. Here the faculty eat, and quite well. If the students are having roast beef, the professors dine on prime rib. If the students get steak, faculty members feast on filet mignon. Everyone wears an academic gown while eating. The meal begins with a prayer (in Latin).

Whatever is served, you can cut the pretense with a knife. None of this is a problem, of course, if you don't take yourself too seriously—in fact, it can be great fun. Unfortunately, in that environment, some people are tempted to take themselves far too seriously.

That night the chaplain introduced Jerry. After the prayer, all took their seats at the high table. A history professor immediately asked, "So, Jerry, why are you a Christian?" Jerry initially thought she was inquiring for personal reasons, though later someone at the table who knew her suggested that she was probably attempting to make the American the night's entertainment. Assuming this was a personal query, Jerry responded without making any kind of philosophical or theological defense of Christian doctrine.

"I am a Christian. I am aware of my failures and shortcomings and the kinds of things the Bible calls sin in my life," Jerry replied. "It is the deep recognition that things are broken and need fixing that has driven me to God for forgiveness. Also, it is out of a deep longing to be loved with a love that does not shy away due to my failures that I have sought this in Christ. I have found that the love and forgiveness of God speak to my deepest need. I have found the gospel, in that regard, compelling."

The historian was clearly taken aback. Perhaps she had been

expecting some kind of rational argument that she could then spend the rest of the meal trying to dissect.

"Well," she said, "I can appreciate what you are saying, but that's just not my issue." Knowing that anyone who has honestly evaluated his or her life must be aware of many personal mistakes and shortcomings, Jerry was surprised by her answer. He thought she was either bluffing or lying to herself.

"I think I understand what you are saying," Jerry responded. "In fact, I became a Christian in my first year in college and didn't become perfect overnight. It took two or three weeks." Getting the joke, everyone at the high table broke out in laughter. When things settled down, he looked at the woman and said, "Your laughter just betrayed you."

"What do you mean?"

"You and I just met, so you couldn't possibly know specifics in my life that make my statement about achieving perfection nothing but nonsense. So your laughter meant that either your read of history or your read of your own struggles revealed this to you."

With a note of humility and honesty, the professor acknowledged, "You got me."

Trusting in the presence of the Lord, Jerry gently pressed his advantage, hoping this woman would become aware of her need for God. "Then knowing of your own struggles in life and the incongruities between what you know you should be and how you actually live, what gets you by when you make an honest assessment of your life?"

"I have faith in humanity!"

"I am eager for anything that will help me grow and get better," Jerry responded, attempting to go as deep as she would let him. "May I ask you a couple of questions about your faith in humanity?"

"Yes."

"Have you ever been wounded by another human being before?"

"Of course!" she said with gusto and perhaps a touch of defensiveness.

"Have you ever wounded another human being?"

The professor's answer was more subdued. "I suppose so." It was clear she was a little softer on herself than on those who had wounded her.

"How does this faith in humanity work," Jerry asked, "when we live in a world where we have been wounded and where we have wounded others?"

At that moment, one of the other Fellows at the high table asked, "How does it work for Christians?" Then the group spent the rest of the evening talking about the love and grace of God. Clearly the Lord was present at the high table that night.

Though we are all wounded, not all of us are broken. But when we acknowledge our brokenness, God is present. He speaks to us in our brokenness that we might discover His power to mend us. We go to Him, unlike Him, and then go out into the world sharing His presence with others. We can expect many people to be on this path of acknowledgment, because brokenness is universal and across time.

AN EXAMINED LIFE

William Wordsworth and many of the Romantics raged against the industrialization occurring in Europe in the early 1800s. They found it painful to watch the England of their childhood becoming covered with soot and smoke. The social problems created when the population began moving from farms into the cramped and troubled cities appalled them. Further, as Wordsworth aged, he found himself longing for the lost innocence of his youth. He wanted the broken bits and pieces restored and longed for the brokenness of his culture to be mended also. Wordsworth's longing tracks with anyone who is truly honest about his or her own brokenness.

We cannot grow without accumulating some weight of regret.

Yet we must help people to see their own role in their brokenness so that they may arrive at the lasting solution, which starts with forgiveness through Christ. But they are unlikely to embrace forgiveness until they acknowledge their *need* for forgiveness. The path to the soul's healing begins with honest self-assessment. As Socrates said, "The unexamined life is not worth living."[2] It is a small jump to move from this understanding to the complementary realization that the examined life will require modifications. The medieval monk who wrote *The Cloud of Unknowing* observed:

> Humility is nothing else but a true knowledge and awareness of oneself as one really is. For surely whoever truly saw and felt himself as he is, would truly be humble. Two things cause humility. One is the degradation, wretchedness, and weakness of man to which by sin he has fallen: he ought to be aware of

this, partially at any rate, all the time he lives, however holy he may be. The other is the superabundant love and worth of God in himself: gazing on which all nature trembles, all scholars are fools, all saints and angels blind.[3]

The truth is: you cannot grow without accumulating some weight of regret. Everyone arrives at moments in life when we realize that paths we chose would have worked out better if we had known more. We recall the selfish acts and unkind words that will not go away and wish we had done what we now know to be true. All growth in knowledge gives us more by which we can evaluate our past acts. Had we known a certain fact earlier, we might have acted very differently.

THE ACTIVE PRESENCE OF GRACE

All of us have made certain decisions, only to realize later how hurtful they were to others, and even to us. Stan has tried to be a good father to his three children, but they are not shy about pointing out his occasional outbursts of temper, his bouts of inattentiveness, and his cutting remarks delivered under stress. Such remembrance brings pain—both to his kids and to Stan.

In the face of this unavoidable pain, you might be tempted to say, "If I cannot grow without regret, then why grow at all?" We'd rather stay curled up in our private caves than face pain. Of course, we all know intuitively why withdrawal is untenable. When we stop growing, we begin to die. We must face the truth and grow in order to stop hurting others and ourselves.

But there is much more to personal growth than pulling ourselves up by our own bootstraps. In truth, we are most likely to grow when we realize the active presence of grace in our lives. We grow best when we know that God loves us. This unbelievably comforting knowledge makes it possible to look honestly at our lives and humbly resign ourselves to His grace and forgiveness. The longing to have one's brokenness fixed may be the very place where God is making His sacramental presence known. The field of the soul is being plowed, the soil turned and made ready to receive the gospel.

This awareness of brokenness, however, can be tricky to negotiate. Some, to be sure, turn from their brokenness and find grace and forgiveness in Christ. But others turn to mere religion in a misguided and ultimately futile attempt to fix their brokenness on their own. Here religion can actually prevent a true encounter with Christ. There were plenty of religious people in Jesus' day, after all, who did not receive what He offered. Perhaps they had learned the art of hiding their insecurities and their deep longing behind a religious mask.

ANSWERING THE CHARGE OF HYPOCRISY

It is easy to do, even in the church, which is supposed to be the community of the redeemed. Yet the easy charge of hypocrisy may distract from deeper issues. Our hypocrisy does not obviate someone else's need for mending. It doesn't even make logical sense.

First, although *many* who claim Christ do not seem to be honestly following Him, it does not necessarily follow that *all* who claim to be Christians are equally false and unfaithful. Second, if we judged any segment of society by its worst examples, who could stand? We will always have bad professors, bad students, bad politicians, bad pastors and priests, and bad journalists. We must look at the healthy example before we can investigate what caused the diseased version.

Third, the charge of hypocrisy may be a place where God is sacramentally present. The hypocrisy charge that seems to shut the door to the gospel may in fact be the very thing that opens the heart to the message of forgiveness and love.

If you answer the charge with this kind of honesty, chances are the response will be equally honest.

The charge of hypocrisy often indicates that the person has been wounded by someone claiming to be a follower of Christ. "Atheists may have an arsenal of arguments against God or religion," author Rob Moll notes. "But at heart, rejection of God seems not to be a purely logical choice against the possibility or desirability of God. Rather, it is often a rejection of God's people."[4]

Yet we know that Jesus Himself said that not all who claim to be His followers are.[5] He warned about the presence of weeds among the wheat.[6]

Nonetheless, the person who charges that all Christians are hypocrites doesn't need a lecture on how to be more discerning. He or she needs an honest answer, and honesty begins with acknowledging the basic truth of the accusation. Here is one way for the sacramental evangelist to do so.

"It is very perceptive of you to see there are hypocrites in the church," we might say, "and you are right. Do you know how I know you are right?"

"No," the critic might respond. "How do you know?"

"Because I am in the church and I am a hypocrite," we might answer. "I believe in the high ideal of love, and yet I've had sharp words with the people I say I love most in this world. I believe in justice, but there have been times when I have been unfair with others. I did not set out to be unfair, but I realized after the fact that I could have done much better in my treatment of other human beings."

If you answer the charge with this kind of honesty, chances are the response will be equally honest. "Well, when you put it like that," the person might admit, "I would have to say that there are inconsistencies in my life, too."

Then, following God's leading, you might follow up with, "As you have become aware of these inconsistencies in your life, what have you found helps you get by or get better?" If the friend says he or she still struggles, then you are simply two pilgrims walking the same road. We are both aware of our shortcomings and brokenness, and we can begin to share personal discoveries.

"I struggle, too," it will probably be appropriate to say. "May I share what I am beginning to discover?" At this point the presence of Christ can and likely will open up the conversation to a discussion of the gospel as a deeply relevant topic.

People want to improve themselves and overcome their failings. They long to repair their brokenness, to become saints, even if they are not conversant with Christian history and theology. Only Christ can provide what they need to get there. Often when people can honestly admit their brokenness, they become willing to admit their need for God's forgiveness and grace. Let's help them do so as we practice the sacrament of evangelism.

Discussion Questions

I. What is the distinction between being wounded (or fallen) and being broken? Do you believe all people are wounded at some point? Are all broken?

2. Are most people aware of their own woundedness? Explain your answer. Have you ever noticed how quick we are to notice the shortcomings of others but how blind we are to our own? Why is this so? Do you think being secure in the love of Jesus could make it easier to see how broken and fallen we truly are?

3. How can you assist in awakening others to their own deep need to have their broken pieces mended? C. S. Lewis suggested that it is being honest about your own brokenness and what you have found in Christ that helps you to mend. What would this look like as you share the good news with others?

4. Do you believe the author of *The Cloud of Unknowing* was right to suggest that two things cause humility: a growing awareness of ourselves as we really are (for whoever truly knew himself as he is would be humble); and a growing awareness of God as He is? Why? Do you believe that humility is a synonym for honesty? Why? Or, why not?

5. How do honesty and humility put us on the same road with others on their pilgrim journey to find God? Why is one of the best ways to communicate being continually mindful of our own daily need for God's love, forgiveness, and grace?

Look for them—there are many examples of longings awakened by the world that allow the sacramental evangelist to begin a conversation that can point to Christ.

15) OTHER LONGINGS

While he was a student at Wheaton College, Todd Beamer had attended a Bible study at Jerry's house. Some years later, when he was thirty-two, Beamer awoke in the relative security of his own home and raised his head from a pillow where it would never come to rest again. He left home to fly off to a business meeting. It was September 11, 2001.

Later that morning the world watched in horror as terrorists flew passenger jets into New York's World Trade Center and into the Pentagon just outside the nation's capital. A short time later, heroic passengers aboard another flight, United Flight 93, confronted Islamic fanatics in the cockpit and prevented them from using the jet as a weapon against the White House or the U.S. Capitol. One of the heroes that day was Beamer, who right before the confrontation famously said, "Let's roll!" In the struggle that ensued, the plane crashed in a Pennsylvania field, killing all aboard.

After that horrible day, Jerry thought often about Beamer, his wife, Lisa, and their two boys. He was not alone in asking, "How can we be safe in this world?" This question points to a ubiquitous longing that only God can fully satisfy.

LONGING FOR SAFETY

We have never been guaranteed safety in this world. C. S. Lewis noted in a sermon, "Learning in War-Time,"[1] that war does not increase death. Lewis could just as easily have noted that disease does not increase death, nor does aging, nor do accidents. How could he make such a claim? Lewis rightly understood that death is total in every generation. One out of one dies! The world has *never* been safe. Nothing in life but our short-sighted vanity suggests that anyone can avoid the fact that existence is a fragile enterprise.

What can this dogged determination to find meaning in a supposedly meaningless universe possibly indicate?

So why do we *expect* to experience perpetual safety? Perhaps we unwisely extrapolate from the fact that most people, most of the time, live in relative safety. Nevertheless, in our saner moments we understand that no one is ever absolutely in the clear. We all know of people who, at the height of their strength, died suddenly: the athlete who collapsed during a basketball game, the soldier who died in his sleep, the healthy young woman in a car accident. It is an old story. After conquering most of the known world, Alexander the Great died in the palace of Nebuchadnezzar II in 323 BC at the age of thirty-two of unknown causes. If even the mightiest succumb, what hope is there for the rest of us?

Perhaps, then, the longing for safety percolates from deep inside of us, revealing a longing rooted in the desire for heaven, the one place where unending safety is perfectly rational. This longing for security, properly understood, may be a built-in pointer to God and a useful tool for the sacramental evangelist in introducing others to Christ.

LONGING FOR MEANING

On 9/11, people asked other questions. These questions reveal layers of longing that may indicate God's active and gracious presence. In a world where many people see life as simply the chaotic product of time and chance, many caught themselves asking, "What does all this mean?" or, "What will this come to mean for us?" We long to make sense of our experiences. What does this tell us? If, as many today claim, there is no meaning in life, then we would never know it, nor would we even desire to make sense of things.

Interned in a Nazi concentration camp, Viktor Frankl lost most of his family, including his young wife. But Frankl survived and sought desperately to make sense of the horror. In his book *Man's Search for Meaning*, the well-known psychiatrist observed, "If there is a meaning in life at all, then there must be meaning in suffering."[2] Certainly in the midst of suffering and crisis, making sense of things may elude us. But we keep coming back to the tragedies of our lives in a never-ending quest to make sense of them.

What can this dogged determination to find meaning in a supposedly meaningless universe possibly indicate? While we are not suggesting that it means only one thing in particular, we do believe it provides a strong indication that some reason for that longing must exist. Certainly existence cannot be the utter chaos some want us to believe. Even their attempt to communicate in meaningful terms their belief that there is no meaning is a contradiction that undercuts their position and muddies the quest to find an answer.

Could it not be possible that we seek to make sense of our experiences because there is a God whose existence allows us to make sense of life? The sacramental evangelist can begin to cultivate these inborn questions to help direct others to Jesus. The process will not be easy. Our world is broken, and we face many thorny issues. But they can awaken questions that might lead people to God.

After 9/11, churches were filled with people looking for comfort and answers. They came to church of their own free will; we Christians did not have to go looking for them. Unfortunately, after a short time, many left. Few were met at the level of their soul-searching questions. In a time of crisis many may have concluded that the church was irrelevant, or perhaps they were looking for quick fixes and instant comfort.

> The sacramental evangelist must work with the material God has already built into the hearts of men and women.

Yet many people face perplexing difficulties in life and are very open to hear what we have to say. Sacramental evangelists can and must read these promptings of the heart, these anguished cries for answers, as God-given. We work with God when we compassionately speak hope into the hearts of men and women who are looking for answers.

LONGING FOR GLORY

God speaks to people through many different longings—even those that we rarely see as good. For example, our oft-selfish desires for fame and fortune are evidence that we were made for something more, and at some level know it. Thomas Traherne, the seventeenth-century English mystic poet, once observed,

> The noble inclination whereby man thirsteth after riches and dominion, is his highest virtue, when rightly guided; and carries him as in a triumphant chariot, to his sovereign happiness. Men are made miserable only by abusing it. Taking a false way to satisfy it, they pursue the wind.[3]

Afraid that people will become ensnared in their own selfish lusts, we tend to tell them that they ought not have such desires. Traherne, however, says the problem is not with the desire *per se* but rather with the inappropriate object of the desire. Traherne understood that God Himself has placed these desires in our hearts so that we will seek their satisfaction in Him. Of course, this means that some people—many, perhaps—will settle for false substitutes. But if someone chooses to pursue riches and power rather than God, it is not the desire that has gone afoul but the person's choice of a "false infinite."

Money and power can never satisfy our deepest yearning. Only God can do that. The sacramental evangelist must work with the material God has already built into the hearts of men and women. When you meet someone whose gods seem to be money and power, don't simply quote the Scripture saying that we cannot serve God and money.[4] That can come later. Instead, try to find out if material things are actually fulfilling this person's longings. Some gentle questioning may help him or her to pause and take spiritual stock. Earthly objects can awaken desire but cannot satisfy it. Pointing this out does not squelch the desire; it merely nudges it toward its proper object.

What other desires might the sacramental evangelist work with? There are many human longings, and this chapter is in no way exhaustive. Perhaps the following examples will reveal some possibilities.

THE TRUE, THE GOOD, AND THE BEAUTIFUL

Plato recognized that for eons men and women have longed for the True, the Good, and the Beautiful. We will briefly consider them in turn here.

We long for the *true* not only to gain academic knowledge. There is, after all, more than one kind of knowledge. We long for the authentic. We want the scoliosis of our lives to measure up to the plumb line of reality. Years ago Jerry heard someone ask John Stott, the eminent pastoral theologian, how Christians can reach postmodernists for Christ. Stott answered, "You will reach the postmodernist by being an authentic person." When Jerry heard this, he went immediately into existential despair. Why? Because *none* of us is an authentic person. We sense the disparity between our convictions and our practices.

In that moment it dawned on Jerry that there has been only one completely authentic person. Only one person in human

192

history has been able to say, "I have lived without any flaws or deficiencies, exhibiting true humanity." That thought led to a new question: "How does an inauthentic person begin to approximate authenticity?" Perhaps we should simply 'fess up to our inauthenticity. There is something true, honest, and unpretentious about this approach. People looking for true authenticity may take note of our honesty and see the God who walks with us.

In a world of compromises and inconsistencies, of nightly newscasts that reveal hypocrisies in our politicians and public figures, the longing for the *good* is never far from the surface. Years ago a woman named Virginia and her husband were expecting their first child. Doctors, however, said the kidneys of the unborn baby were pocked with cysts. They said the child could not possibly live more than a few hours and advised Virginia to abort.

Virginia was heartbroken but also committed to do the good. "I do not know why God chose me to be the mother of this child," she replied, "but since He did I will give birth to this child and I will love it with mother-love the best I can for as long as it lives." So the baby was born. For the little time that remained, Virginia sat in a rocking chair, nursing, holding, and singing songs to the child. There are no scales to measure such love and courage.

A person sensitive to beauty can speak explicitly into areas where God may be wooing implicitly through art or the natural world.

Years later a woman told Jerry that another set of doctors told her daughter that the baby she was carrying would die hours after birth, and they too advised an abortion. Jerry's friend asked, "What do I tell my daughter?" Jerry told her about Virginia, who then spoke with this woman's daughter on the phone every week. Taking courage from Virginia's example, the daughter chose to give mother-love to her child for as long as that child should live. After the baby was born, the doctors discovered that they had made a misdiagnosis. The baby was fine.

It is a remarkable story. It is a story about goodness. We long to be united with such goodness, to know that it exists and that it can be embodied in our experience. The quest for the good may be an indicator that God is creating a thirst in someone's heart. The sacramental evangelist can speak to that issue, working with God to make explicit what God is doing implicitly.

People also long for *beauty*. We sense it when creation awakens after a long winter. In Chicago, home of the many months' long winter, we note with wonder the crocuses as they pop through the melting snow. We feel awe when rediscovering the golden daffodils, whose trumpetlike shape heralds the coming of spring. Our eyes dance with delight as we notice the glorious magenta of the rhododendron and the riotous colors of the tulips. We cannot help but notice as the redbuds, crab apples, and Bradford pears awaken after dormancy.

We lose ourselves in the creative genius that produced a painting, only to realize we've been occupying the best spot in the art museum, unwittingly preventing others from having the same experience. We back up to look longer, still thirsty to see more, only to discover that the museum has provided a bench, because many others have had a similar experience here.

In other words, while there may be some subjectivity about beauty, there is also something very objective about it. And, if beauty is not merely arbitrary and more than one person can have a similar aesthetic experience, then it may be that Someone is speaking to our hearts through the beauty itself. A person sensitive to beauty can speak explicitly into areas where God may be wooing implicitly through art or the natural world. As David Taylor has said,

> We certainly must continue to declare Jesus as the Good Way and the True Truth. But he is not these alone. Jesus is also a Desirable Beauty, one who attracts us by the beauty of his person and works. And he has placed a deep longing in all humans for beauty. When you and I welcome the in-forming, re-forming presence of beauty into our gospel—our evangelism and social action, our worship and work, our praying and playing—we allow beauty to do something that only it can do: generate longing, a longing that is satisfied supremely in the Source of all created beauties, Jesus Christ. And this is very good news.[5]

Remember, we cannot *take* Jesus to anyone. He is already present with every person, ministering grace without regard to individual responsiveness. And no one is beyond the scope of God's love and grace. No one is unloved. There are only tragic figures who, in spite of God's love, resist Him. Nevertheless, as long as people have breath in their lungs, God is demonstrating His grace at some level. We do not always see who is on the verge of responding, and that is all right. None of us would have predicted that Saul, the killer of Christians, would have turned to God. Ananias certainly didn't, but he left his imperfect knowledge in the hands of the Lord, who sent him to minister to a man who became the great theologian and missionary of the church.[6]

Since God is at work with each person we meet, it is wise to participate with Him in wooing others to Himself. The sacramental evangelist, increasingly sensitive to the presence of Christ, will cultivate an equal sensitivity to the many ways God may already be speaking.

There are many other examples of longings awakened by the world that allow the sacramental evangelist to begin a conversation that can point people to Christ. Look for them. Watch for a deeper point of connection. It may be the pilgrim longing, the lover longing, the ascetic/saint longing, or one of the longings mentioned in this chapter. Or it could be something different, but the key is to be alert and attentive. God will do the rest.

Discussion Questions

I. If this world is unpredictable and not necessarily safe, why do we long for safety? How did the expectation of safety arise in us if this world cannot deliver on the expectation? Could this paradox be a signal that this longing points us toward a transcendent solution? How can this longing be a tool for sharing the gospel with others?

2. Why do we long to make sense of our experience? If there is no meaning in life, why should we care to find meaning and significance? Where does this longing come from, and how can we use it to connect heart longing with the gospel?

3. When you see people in pursuit of money or power, is your first impulse to tell them that they ought not to have those desires? Why? Perhaps it would be better to encourage the desires that set them in quest of money and power but to ask the more significant question of whether the money and power have satisfied them. Then ask if they might be looking for something more. What might this kind of conversation look like among your friends and peers?

4. What kind of longing does beauty create in you? Is it likely to affect others in a similar way? Why do you think this may (or may not) be so? How can the quest for beauty be a means of connecting the gospel to the deep longings of a person's heart?

5. What other kinds of longings can you think of that might prove significant in exploring with others in order to point them to Christ? How could you use these longings as tools to make the point that the heart's deepest longing is for God?

PART 4

CONTENT

AND FOLLOW-UP

16. Who We Are

17. Communication

18. Follow-Up #1: Jesus, Prayer, and Bible Study

19. Follow-Up #2: Worship, Fellowship, Obedience, and Stewardship

20. Reproducing Reproducers

Why is theology important?

Because it helps us see that

the gospel really is good news.

16) WHO WE ARE

Jean Twenge, a professor of psychology at San Diego State University, wrote *Generation Me*, detailing the narcissism that besets many young people. In it she notes that 91 percent of teens described themselves as responsible, 79 percent rated themselves as very intelligent, and 74 percent believed themselves to be physically attractive.[1] The survey is reminiscent of Garrison Keillor's *Lake Wobegon*, "where all the children are above average."

Down through church history, there have been two diametrically opposed views about the nature of mankind. On the one hand, we can inflate the idea of our goodness and find ourselves unable to account for human depravity. On the other, however, we can talk up our depravity and denigrate human dignity. Given Twenge's research, it's not hard to see which temptation is most powerful in the present era. This dispute, however, is of more than armchair interest to the sacramental evangelist.

There is no doubt the Scriptures teach that we are inherently sinful, and passages such as the following support this understanding:

And since they did not see fit to acknowledge God, God gave them up to a debased mind to do what ought not to be done. They were filled with all manner of unrighteousness, evil, covetousness, malice. They are full of envy, murder, strife, deceit, maliciousness. They are gossips, slanderers, haters of God, insolent, haughty, boastful, inventors of evil, disobedient to parents, foolish, faithless, heartless, ruthless. Though they know God's decree that those who practice such things deserve to die, they not only do them but give approval to those who practice them.[2]

So of course we acknowledge the reality of human sin, but we also need to realize that this passage does not teach that we are "sinful by nature," as some theologians would have it. Romans 1, while describing some horrific characteristics of human sin, nevertheless does not say that we were created as sinful beings. The Bible, in fact, says that we were created good but fell into debilitating sin by our own choice.

CAN HUMANITY IMPROVE?

Human beings are now, to use a common expression, "damaged goods." But nothing is defined by virtue of its damaged condition, because that implies a time when it was undamaged. If you see a smashed car by the side of the road, you do not assume it was manufactured that way. You assume something bad happened to make it that way. The Bible is clear that something bad happened to make us the way we are.

On the other hand, some would have us believe that humanity is without moral flaw. They would say any problems in people come not from our nature but our environment. Russell Kirk summarizes the views of radicals such as Jean-Jacques Rousseau at the end of the eighteenth century about the nature of humanity thusly:

> Man naturally is benevolent, generous, healthy-souled, but in this age is corrupted by institutions. . . . Mankind, capable of infinite improvement, is struggling upward toward Elysium, and should fix its gaze always upon the future.[3]

This mind-set persists today, despite the evidence. It seems naïve in a world where locks are on the door of every home and car; Internet accounts are password-protected; jails are built to keep criminals off the streets; and wars and rumors of wars abound. Merely scanning the headlines reminds us of the nature of the world we inhabit.

OUR GOODNESS *AND* DEPRAVITY

We can account for humanity's goodness *and* depravity by saying that man, made good, chose to rebel against God and brought evil upon himself. While we are created in the image of God, our ability to reflect that image has been defaced because all aspects of who we are have been infected by sin. Evil is a perversion of the good, but it does not define man's essence.

All this matters for the sacrament of evangelism. What you think about the nature of humanity affects your theology in at least four areas. These in turn affect how we approach people with the good news.

1. *Theology proper.* What we believe about mankind affects our understanding of God. If humanity is essentially and necessarily bad, then God would have had to make us so. This, however, contradicts the holiness and love of God. Since God is both holy and good, we were created to reflect His holiness and goodness.

All of this is good, but it is not *salvific* good; that is, none of these acts, good in themselves, is capable of earning salvation for the person who performed it.

2. *Christology.* Christians assert that the second person of the Trinity, God the Son, became a man. The doctrine of the incarnation, that Jesus Christ took on human life and lived among us in the flesh, is settled orthodoxy. Yet Christians also assert that Jesus was without sin. But if sin is essential to what it means to be human, then Jesus would either be (1) a sinner Himself or (2) not fully human. If either of these is true, He would not have been able to die a substitutionary death for others.

3. *Biblical anthropology.* Scripture offers four categories of mankind: (1) Adam and Eve before the fall were without sin and yet human. (2) Adam and Eve and their progeny (including those regenerated by God's grace) are infected by sin. (3) Christ in His sinless humanity. (4) Man in his glorified state in heaven, with his sin eradicated but not his humanity.

In only one of these four categories is sin present, so sin cannot be the defining characteristic of what it means to be human.

4. *Soteriology.* Our view of humanity determines our view of salvation. If you see a pig wallowing in the mud, you do not kick the pig and tell him he shouldn't live like that. He is living accord-

ing to his nature. In the same way, one could argue that if you see a person living a life of dissipation, intemperance, crime, and betrayal, you should leave him alone because he's just living according to his nature. But we do not leave an individual in a state of dissipation. The proclamation of the gospel is testimony to the fact that man is not living according to his nature. He needs rescue. Lost sinners cannot clean up their acts and save themselves. That requires God's grace in Christ. Christians believe this grace is only available through Christ's work on the cross in which, once for all, He made God's forgiveness available to all who believe.

Clearly, then, we know that mankind:

is good *by* nature, and now possesses a nature infected by sin.

Thus, even though we are sinners, we have inherent dignity. These characteristics are true of all people everywhere, and they are the reason nations where Christianity has deep roots will provide a fair trial to the worst of criminals. No matter how far an individual plunges into the depths of human depravity, the attempt at a fair trial reflects our belief in the dignity of mankind. The fact that crimes occur at all is testimony that something has gone horribly awry in what God created as good.

THE NATURE OF HUMANITY

And yet we must grapple with the undeniable fact that even though mankind is inherently bad, those who are unregenerate are capable of great good. When Jerry started first grade, a third of the members of his class wore polio braces. We no longer see polio braces on children because a nonbelieving physician, Jonas Salk, discovered the preventive vaccine for the disease. This fact is no problem for the believing Christian, because we have it on the authority of Jesus Himself that any person can be a conduit of God's common grace. Jesus said, "If you then, who are evil, know how to give good gifts to your children . . ." (Luke 11:13).

It is true that Paul said, "For I know that nothing good dwells in me, that is, in my flesh. For I have the desire to do what is right, but not the ability to carry it out" (Romans 7:18). Is this a contradiction? Not at all. Jesus and Paul are addressing separate issues. Jesus recognizes that fallen human beings are capable of giving good, beneficial gifts to others. History is replete with examples of people who have sacrificed for their children; soldiers who have smothered hand grenades to protect their comrades; engineers who have labored hours to make the lives of others less toilsome; contractors who have built dams to prevent flooding and provide energy and clean water for millions. All of this is good, but it is not *salvific* good; that is, none of these acts, good in themselves, is capable of earning salvation for the person who performed it. That is what Paul is talking about.

Therefore, we must understand that people are not created sinful. We are made in the image of God,[4] or *Imago Dei*. That image, though corrupted at the fall,[5] is not lost. As John Calvin writes, ". . . the depravity and wickedness, whether of man or the devil, and the sins thence resulting, being not from nature, but from the corruption of nature."[6]

Later Calvin writes, "Although we grant that the image of God was not utterly effaced and destroyed in him, it was, however, so corrupted, that anything which remains is fearful deformity; and, therefore, our deliverance begins with that renovation which we obtain from Christ, who is, therefore called the second

Adam, because he restores us to true and substantial integrity."[7]

What then do we Christians mean when we speak of the doctrine of original sin? Original sin has been called "the only empirically verifiable doctrine of the Christian faith."[8] That is, we see its evidence everywhere in the world and throughout human history. Sin not only infects us in our bad acts but also in our good ones. When we do something good, who among us is not tempted to selfishly toot our own horn to say, "Look at me"?

Yet sin is not original to creation, because it entered the world *after* creation. Rather, it is as original as the first club foot or the first case of cancer or gangrene. It is as original as the first murder, the first case of pedophilia, or the first act of torture. These horrors are all consequences and actions that *followed* Adam and Eve's rebellion. Sin is original in the sense that there was a time when it did not exist, and now that it does, it has spread to all people. Sin had a definite beginning and has a definite scope.

The doctrine of original sin is not an attempt to ascribe blame ("Is sin Adam's fault or mine?") but rather an explanation of a universal phenomenon—that all are prone to sin. All of us have a propensity to moral deficiency; we all tend, at some level, to live beneath our own moral aspirations, much less God's. If we are sinners, and if our sin is offensive to a holy God, and if our sin has affected us totally, then we can do nothing to repair the damage. We are left to God's mercy and are hopeless without His grace.

THE KINDNESS OF GOD

And if every part of us is infected, then this includes our reason. This mental infection means we cannot think our way out of our depravity. Our sin also includes our volition, which means we cannot repair our condition by sheer willpower. If our emotions are affected, we cannot feel ourselves free from our sin. The Scriptures say unequivocally that "you were dead in the trespasses and sins."[9] If we are dead, then we can do nothing to enliven ourselves. Just as those who are physically dead cannot respond to physical stimuli, so too those who are spiritually dead cannot respond to spiritual stimuli.

Salvation is not conditioned by anything we can do. God is no man's debtor. His actions are not conditioned by our behavior. God's creatures may benefit from His acts, but they are not the cause of what He does. God does not reason the way His creatures do, either. He doesn't begin with propositions and then reason His way to a conclusion. He has never needed to have a new idea. His knowledge is immediate; as the ancients said, He has *vision*. He has known throughout eternity those who would be His.

Charles Spurgeon is reported to have said, "I believe the doctrine of election, because I am quite certain that, if God had not chosen me, I should never have chosen Him; and I am sure He chose me before I was born, or else He never would have chosen me afterwards."[10] Those who decline to choose God's only way to heaven will have no ground to complain about hell, and those who deserve hell cannot boast if they get to heaven. No one in hell will have a case in saying, "I got here because God was unjust," and no one in heaven will say, "I got here by virtue of my cleverness and self-effort."

Yet what are we to do with the fact that God does not choose all for salvation? Is He ultimately unfair, as some would charge? We need to keep in mind that the grace of God already is extended to all. Christ died for all,[11] but not all respond to Christ's sacrifice. The offer is universal, but His death is only sufficient for those who are overwhelmed by the mercy of God and respond.[12] These people find the grace of God irresistible. This does not mean that God does not extend His grace to all in some way. Every moment in a sinner's life, in a world God has made, demonstrates His grace. Every moment judgment does not fall on an unresponsive or rebellious society exhibits His grace.

The Scriptures remind us that God allows life-giving rain to fall on the just and the unjust.[13] He provides seasons and harvests to all.[14] The very kindness of God leads to repentance[15]—and all receive of that kindness, but, tragically, not all repent. Others suppress God's truth in their unrighteousness[16] and miss out on the love and kindness of God.

Why is theology important in a book about the sacrament of evangelism? Because it helps us see that the gospel really *is* good news, because by it we are forgiven of our sins, whatever our level of self-esteem. But we will not see the gospel as the good news it is if we do not also see ourselves as the sinners Scripture says we are.

Frederick Buechner wisely observed, "The gospel is bad news before it is good news."[17] C. S. Lewis advised that those who share the gospel must be aware of their own sins. Lewis said the best way to awaken in others their need for forgiveness is for those of us presenting the gospel to be very aware of our own.[18]

This awareness testifies to the sacrament of evangelism. That's because our need for Christ is not casual; it is constant. Because we need Him all the time, we can be aware of Him all the time, too. Jesus is with us, always mediating His grace to us. Aware of His grace in our lives, we can speak about it with conviction and joy to others who also need it.

Discussion Questions

1. Frederick Buechner once observed that before the gospel can be good news it must first be bad news. What is the bad news of the gospel? How then does it become good news?

2. When Christians say humanity is sinful, what do they mean?

3. The doctrine of man's depravity does not mean people are incapable of good; it means they are incapable of doing anything that will merit favor with God—that is, they can do nothing to save themselves. What is the only way someone can be forgiven of sin and have a relationship with God?

4. Christians believe it is grace alone that makes them right with God and that God has given this kind of grace freely. If the gospel invites people to consider that God loves them and forgives them, who, in his or her right mind, would ever refuse such an offer?

5. If man is sinful and if he cannot rescue himself from his own, self-made predicament, how important are the love, grace, and forgiveness of God? How did God most dramatically exhibit His grace to you? How can this grace begin to transform you?

Evangelism is primarily about introducing people to the God who is already present; it is not about being perfect.

17) COMMUNICATION

Once the great nineteenth-century preacher and social reformer D. L. Moody was speaking with a critic who told him that he didn't like his method of evangelism. "I don't really like mine all that much, either," Moody replied evenly. "What's yours?"

The man answered that he didn't have one. Moody said in a deadpan reply, "Then I like my way better than yours."[1]

Moody was right. It's better to have a flawed, imperfect approach than to have no approach at all. As we heard Chesterton say in chapter 2, "If a thing is worth doing, it is worth doing badly." Moody was less concerned about the method and more concerned that people attempt to do God's work in the world. Those doing the work will be more likely to refine their methods, anyway. Those not doing the work will tend to be more willing to critique the methods of others.

Sacramental evangelists are responsible, therefore, not to be perfect in their methods but to be active in sharing. This includes a commitment to improve, which is essential in anything worth doing in life, and especially in the sacrament of evangelism. This chapter will present some basic ideas and methods that will sharpen your practice of the sacrament of evangelism.

> **A**ll of God's thoughts of His creatures are tempered by His love.

Try them out and adapt them to your unique situation, knowing that the Lord goes with you. They are not, however, guaranteed to work at all times or with everyone. Evangelism is primarily about introducing people to the God who is already present; it is not about being perfect. God doesn't need perfection in technique; He doesn't even need perfect motives. Of course, we should seek to refine our methods and purify our motives as we mature in Christ. We will never have it all together, but we can grow as we serve.

These ideas and methods are meant to help you clearly introduce Him and leave the results in His hands. Before we can clearly present the gospel, however, we need to be clear ourselves about its essential elements. This leads naturally to a number of questions:

- How much does a person need to know to come to regenerating faith?
- And, if a new believer has regenerating faith, how can I communicate so that he or she understands that this is a sure word but not a last word?
- How can I present the gospel in a way that encourages the new believer to maintain a level of curiosity, wonder, awe, and worship?

We must point people to the Truth who is with us and with them. We must not point them to our own prejudices and fantasies. Perhaps the information in this chapter will provide answers to these and other questions.

ESSENTIAL THINGS: THE GOSPEL

Many helpful gospel presentations and outlines are available.[2] The one we offer isn't meant to be the last word in evangelism. It may or may not fit you. We will say, however, that it is biblical, straightforward, and proven. If it works for you and your situation, by all means, try it. If it doesn't, try something else. (Just remember to retain the basics of the gospel in any method you use.)

The key is not to find a one-size-fits-all approach but to participate as faithfully as we can in the sacrament. The explanations of the points are not to read aloud to the person with whom you are sharing but to sharpen your thinking.

I. God loves us.

The Bible says that "God is love"[3]—that God embodies and is the source and goal of all true love. At God's core is a beating heart of love. He is the Creator and sustainer of love in its myriad forms. The Greek language speaks of love in many ways and contexts: *eros* (erotic love), *phileo* (brotherly love), and *agape* (self-giving love). Needing nothing from His creatures, God the Creator pours out His *agape* on us simply because He loves us—He desires our best. His love is unconditional and freely given to all.[4] All of God's thoughts of His creatures are tempered by His love.

2. We are estranged from God.

Sin, a choice to go our way rather than God's way, has separated us from Him.[5] This separation is not one in space and time. The finite cannot be separated from the infinite, nor the temporal from the eternal. This separation is a moral and relational one. Sin is manifested in evil acts and attitudes, including indifference to what is good. Created to know and love God, people now live in ignorance and fear of Him. We see Him not as the loving heavenly Father He is, but as a capricious and angry Judge. Our default mode is to run from Him, as we are "dead in . . . trespasses and sins."[6] We want nothing to do with God and will not naturally come to Him.

3. Jesus Christ is God's provision for our sin—through Him we are forgiven and reconciled to God.

Jesus, who is both God and Man, came to live the sinless, God-focused life we were created for, and to die in our place as our substitute.[7] Because He is both loving and holy, God came to us in Jesus Christ. In love He sought to provide a way of escape for us; in holiness He could not overlook sin. In Christ His answer to the dilemma was to sacrifice Himself so that we could enjoy a relationship with God. He is the object of our deepest longings.

4. We are called to put our trust in Christ.

We receive this gift of forgiveness through Christ by placing our faith in Him and His finished work on the cross.[8] At the same time, we must repent of, or turn from, our sins. Repentance involves sadness for those places in my past where I did not choose to follow God and consequently hurt others and hurt myself. Repentence is not wanting to do things my way anymore but trusting God and finding peace by living His way.[9] This is the beginning of a lifelong walk with God as we begin to enjoy His presence and share Him with others.

Now, if more detail is needed, we are ready to use Scripture to emphasize what Christ has done for us, and what we must do in response.

ESSENTIAL THINGS: USING SCRIPTURE

Here is another way to explain the heart of the gospel message with Scripture. Using the following verses to emphasize the key theological points of the gospel, intersperse them with the questions shown. (Try adding emphasis where suggested.) This approach will impress on your hearers that Christ died for *them*, and that they need to appropriate the benefits of His death for themselves.

- 1 Peter 2:24: "He himself bore our sins in his body on the tree, that we might die to sin and live to righteousness. By his wounds you have been healed."

  1. According to this verse, do you know where *your* sins are right now?
  2. If your sins are on Christ, what does that make *you*?
  3. Two thousand years ago, when Christ died on the cross for you—in a sense putting forgiveness in a trust account for you to draw on one day—how many of *your* sins were in the future yet to be committed?
  4. How many did He die for?
  5. What does this make *you*?

- 2 Corinthians 5:21: "For our sake [God] made [Christ] to be sin who knew no sin, so that in [Christ] we might become the righteousness of God."

    1. Why did God make Jesus to be sin?
    2. What did Jesus give, and what did we give?

- 1 John 5:11–12: "And this is the testimony, that God gave us eternal life, and this life is in his Son. Whoever has the Son has life; whoever does not have the Son of God does not have life."

    1. Do *you* have the Son? If so, what else do you have?
    2. If you don't have the Son, what don't you have?
    3. Why do you think God set it up this way?

PERSONAL TESTIMONY

Personalize your message. Tell of your own pilgrimage to Christ. C. S. Lewis's autobiography, *Surprised by Joy: The Shape of My Early Life*,[10] provides a good model. Lewis selected the points he wished to tell of his conversion to Christ out of all the teeming details of his life. Lewis's friend, the physician Robert E. Havard, jokingly referred to *Surprised by Joy* as "Suppressed by Jack," because of all the life details that were omitted.[11] But in this way the book could focus on Lewis's spiritual journey without getting diverted into rabbit trails.

Here is a brief sample testimony, from Stan. Notice that it has the four elements: God's love, our sinful estrangement, Christ's death, and our trust. Remember to note also that it uses them in a natural, unforced way. It does not get bogged down in a lot of details that don't fit the outline, but it does add enough color to make it real. Use it for inspiration as you think about your own testimony. Then articulate your own story. Next, practice your testimony aloud until you feel comfortable sharing it whenever God leads. And be prepared to adapt, add, or omit details as each situation requires.

My birth on August 1, 1961, two months early, did not go well. Only three pounds and eleven ounces, I beat the odds and survived. But for the rest of my life I would carry the burden of cerebral palsy.

Through the years I have often asked "Why?" and it was hard not to feel resentful. Most of the time I felt like an inferior, an outsider, afraid of rejection. And sometimes I *was* rejected.

One night I remember looking up at the countless stars splashed across the silent sky. In the darkness my mother said it was hard to believe that all this could have just happened—but I wasn't so sure. My experience led me to suspect that the universe was cold, indifferent, and meaningless. God, if He existed, was either too busy to care or too weak to help.

But needing *something* to believe in beyond this life, I turned to science fiction, UFOs, and "pyramid power." I also began reading books about the end of the world, and that got me into the Bible.

As I read it, I realized that my life could only have meaning if I were properly related to the God who created me, just as I was. And this was a God I had never expected: One who was personally, painfully involved already.

He came to earth as a Man, Jesus Christ, to live the

perfect life I had failed to live and to voluntarily die on the cross in my place—in short, to pay for my sins—including the bitterness, the self-centeredness, and all the rest.

Moreover, He *understood* my frustrating disability. On His way to the cross, Jesus had publicly stumbled and fallen. I could relate. Suspended between heaven and earth, Christ's weakness was exposed for all to see. And yet because He was raised from the dead, someday I too would be raised, with a powerful new resurrection body. That was an offer I couldn't refuse!

I wish I could say that since receiving Christ all of my insecurities have evaporated, and I no longer have doubts about God's love. But that wouldn't be honest. My disability has shaped not just my body but also my soul. Even though I now sense God's presence daily, it will probably take me the rest of my life to overcome my insecurities—but, slowly, I'm getting there!

One day, Jesus' disciples asked, "Rabbi, who sinned, this man, or his parents, that he was born blind?" The Lord said that the man's disability presented a divine opportunity, "that the works of God might be displayed in him."

Undoubtedly I will face more frustrations and heartaches. Yet today I can accept my disability in a way I never could before, because Christ's power is most clearly seen *not* in my strength but in my *weakness*.

ESSENTIAL THINGS: THE INVITATION

As we have said, in the sacrament of evangelism you don't have to force matters. God is always present, and He has a way of making His presence known. We don't have to "make the sale." God's Spirit will do that. We do, however, need to be sensitive and open to His leading. Early in a relationship we may sense that the time is not yet to ask a friend to make a decision—such as with Jerry gently speaking with Brad, the restaurant owner, week after ordinary week.

Yet there are times when it is entirely appropriate and necessary to ask people to make a decision. People make decisions all the time—what to wear, what to major in, whom to marry, whether to buy this house or that one, and so on. We don't expect them in other areas of life to always gather information and never come to a conclusion. At some point they must decide. Even not deciding is a decision, isn't it? So we are merely helping people clarify their own thinking about the God who is near, not convincing them with a slick sales pitch. But clarify they must. Do they believe, or not? As Joshua told the wavering Israelites, "Choose this day whom you will serve."[12]

The sacramental evangelist is doing nothing more than allowing people to do what they already do naturally: choose.

So how do we bring closure to a conversation about God and the gospel? How do we invite a person to make a decision for Christ? Here are some options.

1. Ask God to show you an opportunity for closure. If the person is ready, God will let you know.

2. If you're not sure how to proceed, use a tried and true method.
   a. Campus Crusade for Christ's Circles[13]
   b. The Navigators' Bridge[14]
   c. Evangelism Explosion's two questions[15]
      (1) If you were to die tonight, do you know for certain that you would go to heaven?
      (2) If you died tonight and stood before God and He asked, "Why should I let you into My kingdom?" what would you tell Him?[16]

ESSENTIAL THINGS: THE CHOICE

One of the glories of being alive and made in the image of God is the capacity to decide. Choice in our culture has been elevated to an almost mystical status. People expect to have the right to choose, and the sacramental evangelist is doing nothing more than allowing them to do what they already do naturally: choose.

Evangelistic preachers almost always have an altar call. They ask people to make a decision—or to make public the decision they have already made in their hearts. Why? Simply because God seems to work when they do.

Stan used to work at Wheaton College's famous Billy Graham Center. In his three years there, he only had the opportunity to see the renowned preacher in the flesh one time. Graham and his team had scheduled a June crusade at the RCA Dome in Indianapolis, and Stan and other BGC staffers and family members were invited to ride down in a chartered bus from the Chicago area to attend.

That warm night Graham, who was getting well on in years, needed help to get to the podium. His youth and energy were things of the past, yet his commitment to see people come to Christ was undimmed. His message, as always, was simply about our need to trust Christ. Truth be told, the sermon was not notable for its erudition, and Stan quickly forgot it.

But he didn't forget Graham's simple but powerful invitation at the end—and the thousands of people who streamed forward in response. Mothers, daughters, fathers, and sons came down to floor level as the music for "Just as I Am" played. The Holy Spirit, working through the prayers, preparation, preaching, and invitation, was palpably present, and people responded. He will make His presence known through us, too.

We have the joyous responsibility to call on people to come forward and trust Christ—if not in an arena, at least in their hearts. To be effectual, however, this trust will manifest itself not just in a onetime decision but in a lifetime of consecrated service. Malcolm Muggeridge once said that a true decision for Christ is not like jumping through a hoop, once; rather, it is deciding to make every decision for Him from here on out.[17] Helping people do so is the subject of our next two chapters.

Discussion Questions

I. You do not need to communicate a formula when presenting the gospel, but it is good to have some kind of outline of the message clear in your mind. What would your basic method be and how might you adjust it to fit circumstances without compromise?

2. What are the essential points to make when communicating the gospel? Why are these points essential?

3. What Scriptures would you use in sharing the gospel? Why?

4. Practice describing how you came to Christ with someone. Keep it brief but make the gospel clear.

5. Why is it so important to give others an opportunity to trust Christ? How would you go about inviting someone to make a decision? Can you think of several ways you might do this? What would they be?

It is important for the sacramental evangelist to help the new Christian to begin knowing Jesus better.

18) FOLLOW-UP #1: JESUS, PRAYER, AND BIBLE STUDY

Ask people to describe what eternal life is like and they may throw out clichés such as sitting on a cloud or strumming a harp . . . forever. Sounds pretty boring, doesn't it? Well, the good news is that eternal life will never be tedious. How can we be so sure, since we have never been to heaven? We can say this with full assurance because eternal life is not primarily about a place but a Person.

Yes, every believer in Christ has the assurance of sins being forgiven and the hope of everlasting life. The Scriptures are unequivocal about this.[1] Delightfully, this eternal life is not merely a quantitative possession (endless time in heaven)—it has qualitative features as well. It is a life *in relationship with Jesus* . . . forever. "And this is eternal life, that they know you the only true God," Jesus prayed to God the Father, "and Jesus Christ whom you have sent."[2]

Thus, it is important for the sacramental evangelist to help the new Christian to begin knowing Jesus better. If eternal life is not primarily a place we go or something that happens to us after we die, but actually *starts the moment we believe*, then the adventure of knowing Christ can begin right now. Follow-up begins with centering a person in Jesus.

JESUS IDENTIFIES WITH US

Because He became a man, Jesus, "very God of very God,"[3] nonetheless can identify with us. Before beginning His short public ministry, Jesus lived a rigorous life as a Palestinian carpenter. It is possible that His earthly father, Joseph, who is not mentioned in the biblical narrative about Jesus in the temple at age twelve, died young. Jesus, being the oldest child, would have had to provide for the family.

Jesus must have experienced the struggles and setbacks of a world where most people barely eked out a living. This is the One we get to know, the One who knows us, who entered our world and feels the ups and downs of life as we actually live it. He is also the One, being God who became man, who can guide us through life's complexities.

THE ATTRACTION OF JESUS

People were drawn to Him. When it was time to call His disciples, Jesus went down to the docks and shouted, "Follow me!" And rough-and-tumble men immediately left their nets and livelihoods.[4] His call was imperious, His authority compelling. Once, when the religious leaders sent soldiers to arrest Him, they returned empty-handed. When the scribes and Pharisees demanded to know why, they answered, "No one ever spoke like this man!"[5] Another time a hostile crowd faced off with Jesus and drove Him to the edge of a cliff. But He looked at them, the crowd parted, and He walked right through them, unscathed.[6]

Crowds were awed by Jesus. Matthew reports that they were "astonished at his teaching, for he was teaching them as one who had authority, and not as their scribes."[7] After a day of instructing a multitude out in the open air, He took compassion on the crowd and said to His disciples, "Give them something to eat."[8] The disciples could only muster up a boy's lunch of five loaves (actually, not much more than dinner rolls) and two fish. For Jesus it was enough. He had the multitude sit in orderly groups; He blessed the fish and loaves; and everyone ate until full. There has never been anyone like Him!

Once in a boat with His disciples on the Sea of Galilee, Jesus was sleeping. A "great storm" came out of nowhere. When His frightened friends awoke Him, Jesus spoke a word and calmed the raging sea. "What sort of man is this," they marveled, "that even winds and sea obey him?"[9] He made the blind to see. He made the lame to walk. His word turned the ulcerated skin of lepers as smooth as a newborn's. He could confront the toughest critics and yet find room on His lap for children. He was bold and gentle. It is the same today. When His followers immerse themselves in His goodness, they can stand up to anything the world throws at them.

Jesus' teaching was compelling and His acts were convincing, but His claims stand apart. One day He claimed to do what only Deity can do:

And when he returned to Capernaum after some days, it was reported that he was at home. And many were gathered together, so that there was no more room, not even at the door. And he was preaching the word to them. And they came, bringing to him a paralytic carried by four men. And when they could not get near him because of the crowd, they removed the roof above him, and when they had made an opening, they let down the bed on which the paralytic lay. And when Jesus saw their faith, he said to the paralytic, "Son, your sins are forgiven." Now some of the scribes were sitting there, questioning in their hearts, "Why does this man speak like that? He is blaspheming! Who can forgive sins but God alone?" And immediately Jesus, perceiving in his spirit that they thus questioned within themselves, said to them, "Why do you question these things in your hearts? Which is easier, to say to the paralytic, 'Your sins are forgiven,' or to say, 'Rise, take up your bed and walk'? But that you may know that the Son of Man has authority on earth to forgive sins"—he said to the paralytic—"I say to you, rise, pick up your bed, and go home." And he rose and immediately picked up his bed and went out before them all, so that they were all amazed and glorified God, saying, "We never saw anything like this!"[10]

Jesus said He was the only way to God.

It was a remarkable claim matched by a remarkable display of power.

THE CLAIMS OF JESUS

Jesus made similar claims in other contexts. To His disciples Jesus said, "I am the way, and the truth, and the life. No one comes to the Father except through me."[11] He said He was the only way to God. It was a very narrow claim; some in our society who seem to worship tolerance of everything no matter what it is take exception to Jesus' claims. But aren't all truth claims, in fact, narrow? There is only one right answer when adding a string of numbers. And being off by only a little bit initially can lead to bigger problems later. Aristotle noted, "The least initial deviation from the truth is multiplied later a thousandfold."[12] Whatever one thinks of Jesus' claims, they cannot be false simply because they are narrow. Further, their narrowness, coupled with His free offer of forgiveness, can be seen as an indicator of a wide generosity—if in fact He *is* the *only* way to God.

At another gathering Jesus actually claimed to *be* God:

So the Jews gathered around him and said to him, "How long will you keep us in suspense? If you are the Christ, tell us plainly." Jesus answered them, "I told you, and you do not believe. The works that I do in my Father's name bear witness about me, but you do not believe because you are not part of my flock. My sheep hear my voice, and I know them, and they follow me. I give them eternal life, and they will never perish, and no one will snatch them out of my hand. My Father, who has given them to me, is greater than all, and no one is able to snatch them out of the Father's hand. I and the Father are one."

The Jews picked up stones again to stone him. Jesus answered them, "I have shown you many good works from the

Father; for which of them are you going to stone me?" The Jews answered him, "It is not for a good work that we are going to stone you but for blasphemy, because you, being a man, make yourself God."[13]

Jesus left no ambiguity. His words were unequivocal, and explicit. If all this is true, the narrowness of His claim to be God, to love without condition, and to forgive all of our sins breeds not arrogance but honesty and humility in His followers. There is no need for pretense. He is aware of all our shortcomings; we can be free to own them. This honesty is a first and important step toward Christian growth. He forgives each flaw and failure. When we acknowledge we need Him more than anything or anyone else in this world, we are free to follow Him.

> **P**rayer can include many elements: worship, confession, thanksgiving, requests and petitions for our needs and the needs of others.

The day after Jesus fed five thousand men (and far more than that when you add in the women and children), the people wanted to make Him their king.[14] He saw deeply into their hearts and knew they were looking for an economic savior, an easy meal ticket—one who could feed their stomachs and ease their gnawing pain. At this point He made the people an offer: "I am the bread of life. I offer myself to you. Take me; find your ultimate satisfaction in me. Feed on me; let your life be sustained in me."

This statement was too difficult for His hearers. Most turned to leave Him, even many of His disciples. In one of the tenderest moments of His earthly ministry, Jesus turned to the Twelve and asked, "Will you leave me also?" Peter responded immediately: "Leave you, Lord? Where would we go? You have the words of eternal life."

Jesus makes a similar offer to us. In essence, He asks, "Am I enough for you?" Will we become distracted by things that can never satisfy but over which we can exercise some control? Or will we renounce such control and turn to Him because He is what we need most? The question we must ask: "Is Jesus enough?" If you lose all of the world's goods but have Him, the answer is *Yes*. Jesus is the hidden treasure, the pearl of great price, worth our all.[15] So follow-up with new believers begins by pointing them to Christ. We are to look "to Jesus, the founder and perfecter of our faith."[16]

APPROACHING HIM IN PRAYER

We need to help new believers look to Him by cultivating two habits: *prayer* and *personal Bible study*. These are the foundations of a solid relationship with God. In prayer we speak with God; in His Word, He speaks with us. Through these means we enjoy ongoing dialogue with Him.

Certainly prayer can include many elements: worship, confession, thanksgiving, requests and petitions for our needs and the needs of others. Though these elements are all encouraged in Scripture, they are not the primary reasons to pray. There is something deeper. George MacDonald, whose books deeply inspired C. S. Lewis, wrote:

"But if God is so good as you represent him, and if he knows all that we need, and better far than we do ourselves, why should it be necessary to ask him for anything?"

I answer, What if he knows prayer to be the thing we need first and most? What if the main object in God's idea of prayer be the supplying of our great, our endless need—the need of himself? What if the good of all our smaller and lower needs lies in this, that they help to drive us to God? Hunger may drive the runaway child home, and he may or may not be fed at once, but he needs his mother more than his dinner. Communion with God is the one need of the soul beyond all other need; prayer is the beginning of that communion, and some need is the motive of that prayer. Our wants are for the sake of our coming into communion with God, our eternal need. . . . We must ask that we may receive; but that we should receive what we ask in respect of our lower needs, is not God's end in making us pray, for he could give us every-thing without that: to bring his child to his knee, God with-holds that man may ask.[17]

We pray to know God. In prayer we open our hearts to Him and discover in Him a perfectly safe relationship—*the* perfectly safe relationship. Because He knows all that is on our hearts already, we need hide nothing from Him. We are honest with Him about our needs. As MacDonald rightly notes, all of our lesser needs should drive us to Him, our greatest need. In Him we discover the love that forgives and nurtures us to spiritual health and wholeness.

CONTINUING THROUGH HIS WORD

We also read in order to know Him. The new believer therefore ought also to cultivate a lifelong habit of Scripture study. Believers derive all their hope and encouragement from the Word of God. From the Bible we hear God's assurances of love and grace, through every hour and every step of our lives. No matter our circumstances, the Christian gains perspective by reading and studying God's Word with the help of the Holy Spirit.

In His Word we learn things about Him that we could never learn from the created order.

While there is much we might say about studying God's Word, the apostle Paul gave basic advice to his protégé Timothy that will help all Christians understand why it is so important:

> But as for you, continue in what you have learned and have firmly believed, knowing from whom you learned it and how from childhood you have been acquainted with the sacred writings, which are able to make you wise for salvation through faith in Christ Jesus. All Scripture is breathed out by God and profitable for teaching, for reproof, for correction, and for training in righteousness, that the man of God may be competent, equipped for every good work.[18]

After giving the command to continue in the Scriptures, Paul tells us why. "All Scripture is breathed out by God," he says, which means that it expresses the very character of God. There is no denying, of course, that we can learn much about God from His creation. The psalmist wrote, "The heavens declare the glory of God, and the sky above proclaims his handiwork."[19] Paul wholeheartedly agreed, declaring, "For his invisible attributes, namely, his eternal power and divine nature, have been clearly perceived, ever since the creation of the world, in the things that have been made."[20]

But general revelation, that which is available to all, can only take us so far. We need special revelation—that is, His Word. In it we learn things about Him that we could never learn from the created order, among them, His omniscience, justice, omnipresence, faithfulness, and love.

Paul also says studying God's Word is *profitable.* That is, all who make an investment in it will receive a return. The benefits, according to Paul, include teaching, reproof, correction, and training in righteousness.

Jesus told Nicodemus that he needed to be *born again.*[21] Birth naturally leads to growth. If a baby remained at her birth weight, the result would be tragic. It is just as tragic when a new Christian remains at her spiritual birth weight. We were born again so that we might grow in Christ. And we grow by studying the Word and consuming good *teaching.* As 1 Peter 2:2 tells us, "Like newborn infants, long for the pure spiritual milk, that by it you may grow up into salvation."[22] The Scriptures are necessary to grow; faithful study of the Bible is profitable.

Paul says that the Bible profits us through *reproof.* At first sight this seems rather odd. Reproofs, or scoldings, are painful, and we tend to avoid them. On the other hand, none of us wants to still be where we are today ten years from now. Each of us wants to see personal development, some progress. Each of us carries hindrances to our own spiritual development. We may have blind spots; we may have long-held grudges that corrode our hearts and poison our relationships; we may be flush with insecurities that we seek to anesthetize. The reproofs of Scripture are profitable for those who heed them and are thus set free. Reproofs are the scalpel of God's Word wielded by the Divine Surgeon in the goal of our mending.

The Scriptures also speak to our *correction*. The Greek word for correction literally means "to make straight again." From it we get the English words *orthodontist* (a teeth-straightener), *orthopedist* (a walk-straightener), and *orthodoxy* (straight, or correct, doctrine). If reproof is the scalpel, correction is the healing balm. The corrections of Scripture nurture the Christian toward practices that lead to spiritual maturity.

The Scriptures also *train us in righteousness*. Good living habits are cultivated over time and often involve trouble and sweat. But the sacramental presence of Jesus provides encouragement and forgiveness in the midst of our training. When we have made a mess of things, Christ's love gives us the courage to face how we have hurt others and how we can become better people.

PERSISTENT TRAINING

And this training is not a one and done. One practice session does not make you skilled in a sport, after all. You have to work at it, day after day, week after week, and season after season. Would we expect to do any less in training our souls? As Paul said, "Do you not know that in a race all the runners run, but only one receives the prize? So run that you may obtain it. Every athlete exercises self-control in all things. They do it to receive a perishable wreath, but we an imperishable."[23]

Training is profitable; lack of training can be dangerous. When Jerry was a college freshman, a wrestling coach talked him into joining the team. It seems the wrestler at Jerry's weight had broken his leg that week, and the coach needed someone to take his place. Though Jerry was an athlete, he had never wrestled. He had never even seen a wrestling match.

During Jerry's first collegiate wrestling match, he walked out on the mat and shook hands with his opponent. The referee blew his whistle, and Jerry set the record for the fastest pin in the history of the college. There was just one problem: he was the one being pinned. Seventeen seconds after the match started, he was flat on his back, counting the knot holes on the gym ceiling. Jerry was pinned because he had no training.

Unfortunately, Christians find themselves pinned every day amid temptations, frustrations, and relational struggles because they have no training in the complexities of life. The Word of God, however, can profitably train us in righteousness, in what mature living looks like. The Scriptures guide us to become more like Christ, who walks with us as the founder and perfecter of our faith.

Discussion Questions

I. Following up with a new Christian is vital. How would you begin having regular meetings with this person?

2. If eternal life does not merely speak of the duration of one's existence but also the blessedness of an eternal relationship with Christ, how might you help a new believer cultivate that relationship?

3. What are the most important things to know about Christ in order to fall more deeply in love with Him? How can you communicate them to the new believer?

4. Why is prayer so important in a growing relationship with Christ? What are some essential elements to communicate to a new convert in order that he or she will value a life of prayer?

5. If we speak to God in prayer, we can be confident that He continues to speak to us in Scripture. How can we encourage in a new believer a hunger for God's Word? How could you encourage him or her to develop the habit of regular Bible reading and study?

And whatever we do to glorify
this God, we are to do together,
in Christian fellowship.

19) FOLLOW-UP #2: WORSHIP, FELLOWSHIP, OBEDIENCE, AND STEWARDSHIP

God's sacramental presence often comes mediated through His people. Once Stan found himself suddenly laid off and was in a daze about how God would provide for his family. As he tried to process what was happening through his sudden mental numbness, it began to sink in that he, his wife of twenty-two years, and their three children were suddenly facing a very uncertain future. Then God's people, prompted by the God who is ever-present, went into action.

Christian friends picked up groceries for the Guthries. Another friend bought and installed more memory for Stan's ailing computer. Others gave money, prayed, bought lunch, shared job leads, and helped with résumés. And God provided through these and other means.

Then an MRI brought the unwelcome news that the rotator cuff for Stan's right shoulder, on his good side, was torn and needed surgery. Because Stan depends greatly on his right arm to get around, the prospect of losing full use of it for who knows how long was scary. But amid his fears and frustrations, members of his local church again responded with prayers, meals, rides, house-cleaning, shopping, unexpected gifts, and more. And again the Lord provided in the midst of the trial.

These days it's fashionable to gripe about the shortcomings of one's church. To Stan's embarrassment, he will admit that he's done it more than a few times. But he has also seen this particular body of believers repeatedly spring into action when he has needed it the most. In this way, we can experience Christ through His people.

WORSHIP TOGETHER

In chapter 18 we encouraged you to help new believers get to know Jesus, study God's Word, and be faithful in prayer. There's nothing wrong with any of these actions, of course. But if that's *all* we did, then we would be helping people to develop a very myopic, self-centered, "Just me and Jesus" kind of faith. That's because each of those three elements—knowledge of the Lord, Bible study, and prayer—can be practiced without regard to anyone else.

Discipleship is important work, but it is not lonely work. It is done in the presence of the Holy Spirit and God's people. Therefore it is sacramental work. We are not to be Lone Ranger Christians but members of the divinely ordained people of God.

As God's people, we are called to *worship* corporately, and new believers must be strongly encouraged to take part. "And let us consider how to stir up one another to love and good works," God's

Word says, "not neglecting to meet together, as is the habit of some, but encouraging one another, and all the more as you see the Day drawing near."[1]

One of the Greek words for worship is *proskuneo*. It literally means *to kiss toward*. It conveys a Middle Eastern image of kissing the hand, one's head bowed in reverence. Another New Testament word for worship is *lutreo*, which means *worship through service*. Both have embedded in them the idea of one's responsibility to someone higher. Worship means honoring the honorable. It is an act of justice[2] because it renders what is due. It is because God is great and worthy to be praised that believers gather and worship Him, making this practice one of the rhythms of life.

Worship is essential in cultivating a perpetually high regard for God and a proper humility and honesty in us.

Worship also benefits the worshiper. Entering a place of worship reverently, we begin to experience an overwhelming sense of God's greatness and our smallness. We are weak and dependent, vulnerable and fragile. One hurricane, earthquake, flash flood, tornado, rushing river, or tsunami reveals the truth of this insight. Worship brings us face-to-face with our Creator.

Worship is essential in cultivating a perpetually high regard for God and a proper humility and honesty in us. Corporate worship is prescribed in both testaments. The Scriptures teach that since God took six days to create the universe and rested on the seventh day, we are to set aside a day to worship Him.[3] This is not so that we may receive a dispensation to forget Him the rest of the week, but so that we can't help but remember Him even better during the workweek. The sacramental evangelist's work is not done until he or she nurtures in new Christians a hunger and thirst for worship, wherever they are and whatever activity they may be doing, because Christ is near. As Paul said, "So, whether you eat or drink, or whatever you do, do all to the glory of God."[4]

WALKING TOGETHER

And whatever we do to glorify this God, we are to do together, in Christian *fellowship*. That is because this God has provided the template for fellowship in His own being, as He is eternally existent in three persons: God the Father, God the Son, and God the Holy Spirit. This statement may be difficult for the new believer (not to mention the rest of us) to understand, but it is not illogical. Here's why:

In community, we are shaped and fashioned to become more like Christ.

Christians believe God is noncontingent—that is, that He is self-existent and independent. Nothing accounts for His being or character. Christians believe God's love cannot merely be a by-product of creation or it would be contingent. Relational attributes, such as love, in a noncontingent being presuppose that relationship is in fact necessary in that being.

For the purposes of the new believer, this means that since the Scriptures say that humans are made in the image of God, we are also relational beings, made for community rather than isolation.

Sin, however, estranges us from God and from one another. God's love and forgiveness reconcile us to God and call us back into relationship with one another.

And as we relate with one another, we become aware of our interdependence. Scripture expresses it with a beautiful metaphor: The church is the body of Christ.[5] A body is an organism made up of many organs all functioning together. In a world full of broken relationships, nothing could be more relevant than this: At the core of the universe, a Relationship exists eternally, and we are meant to reflect it. As we worship and serve God, we are brought into community. Like members of an orchestra, we respond to the lead of one Conductor, and we play His music in harmony with one another.

In this community, we are shaped and fashioned to become more like Christ. Such fellowship makes us aware of the sacramental presence of Christ, who mediates grace so that we can appropriate the very practical life skill of harmonious living. Because we are all sinners, this often takes work as we tune ourselves to the triune God.

> **O**bedience enables us to live beyond our inclinations; our lives become far healthier spiritually, emotionally, and relationally.

Fellowship is vital. We need one another. Coals burn together. Remove one and it grows cold. Lack of fellowship cools our faith. Indeed, sharing openly and honestly with one another can help protect us from temptation. But a commitment to fellowship also provides us with a place to confess our sins and be restored, to learn from our mistakes and mature. No new believer who is isolated from others, no matter how passionate, burns long for Christ.

BELIEF IN ACTION

One of the blessings of fellowship is how it allows us to see *obedience* in action. We come to Christ broken and in need of repair. There is so much we do not know or understand. The new believer ought to be able to see a life of obedience in other Christians. The God who designed us knows best how our lives ought to operate. The Bible is God's operating manual, and we need to see other people carrying out its instructions. Stan saw that obedience in the lives of fellow church members.

We cannot hope to grasp obedience on our own, so we need others. But whether we see obedience modeled by others or not, practicing it on our own can also lead us into the sacramental presence of Christ. We may not always understand why God calls us in His Word to do certain things, but we will learn that every act of obedience accesses for us the benefits of omniscience.

That is, when we obey God, though we are limited in our own understanding, we have the capacity to live more wisely than we otherwise naturally would. For example, the Bible says we should forgive those who hurt us. This seems countercultural, counterintuitive, counter-everything that is natural to us. But when we obey and forgive, we can live beyond the bitterness that would otherwise take over our hearts. "To forgive is to set a prisoner free," the late Lewis B. Smedes once said, "and discover that the prisoner was you."[6]

Obedience enables us to live beyond our inclinations; our lives become far healthier spiritually, emotionally, and relationally.

Obedience is the road to freedom. Rousseau wrote in *The Social Contract*, "Man is born free but everywhere we find him in chains."[7] Rousseau saw the "chains" as social custom, religion, tradition, and law, both natural and civil. These, he believed, created a bondage that truncated development and prevented individuals from fulfilling their nature. Many of our modern social ethics find their germination in the seedbed of Rousseau's thought.

Yet Rousseau's presuppositions are preposterous. Throwing off all restraint and doing only what comes naturally leads to intolerable problems. Functioning beyond control is not functioning properly. Obedience to the restraints of just law and heeding the voices of custom and tradition are signs of maturity, not bondage. Just law does not limit freedom. It limits only that form of license that demands for itself more freedom than is proper or fair; the license that asserts one's will at the expense of others.

But contrary to Rousseau, humanity is not the measure of all things. We are sinful and broken people. Reality demands obedience and discipline. Obedience is the splint God places on the broken life in order that it might mend. Discipline is the gymnasium in which the atrophied character gains strength as it internalizes obedience. The sacramental evangelist must nurture the new believer in trusting obedience so that he or she might mend and grow in Christ.

SHARING RESOURCES

A key part of obedience is *stewardship*, the recognition that all we have is a gift from our gracious Lord and ultimately belongs to Him. Some of us have more, some less. It is not for us to complain about whatever state in which we find ourselves. Rather, it is our task to be grateful and to express that gratitude by employing our time, energy, money, and talents in serving Christ and others. The sacramental evangelist should encourage new believers to share their resources so that they can discover the active presence of God in their lives.

During World War II, Dr. Bob Smith, a philosophy professor at Bethel College and Seminary, lived next door to a woman who was a grouch. If Dr. Bob's boys ever crossed even a corner of her yard going down the street to play, Mrs. Kirby shot out of the house to chase them away with a broom. One day when Dr. Bob returned home from a very busy day teaching, his wife told him she saw Mrs. Kirby hanging out her laundry and noticed that the lady's wrists were red and swollen. Mrs. Kirby had explained to her that the roll on her wringer washing machine was broken and she had to wring out all of her laundry by hand.

Dr. Bob went next door and asked Mrs. Kirby if he could take a look at the washer. The next day on his way home from work, he stopped off at a hardware store and bought a new wringer roll. He returned to Mrs. Kirby's house and installed it, and the washer worked fine again. Mrs. Kirby asked what she owed Dr. Bob for the wringer roll. He told her it was a gift. She then asked, "Well, what do I owe you for the labor?" He told her this was also a gift. Not surprisingly, she was touched by these kindnesses.

"Mrs. Kirby," Dr. Bob said, "one day one of my boys is going to be outside playing baseball in the street, and he is going to hit a baseball through that big, beautiful picture window in your living room. When this occurs, I'll come over and clean up the mess and replace your window. In the meantime, please be kind to my boys." From that day on, Mrs. Kirby started baking cookies for the Smith boys and even set aside part of her strawberry patch for them.

The Smiths soon realized that Mrs. Kirby had a hearing problem. One day they saw an advertisement for a two-week free trial offer on an eighty-dollar hearing aid. That was a big chunk of money back then. So Dr. and Mrs. Smith sent away for the hearing aid, which arrived on the day Mrs. Kirby had left to visit her sister two hundred miles away. Wanting to make sure Mrs. Kirby received the benefit of the full two-week trial, they drove the two hundred miles to take the hearing aid to Mrs. Kirby. This was during the time when gasoline was being rationed because of the war.

Mrs. Kirby was stunned to see the Smiths pull up at her sister's home. She was even more shocked that they were willing to purchase the hearing aid for her if she liked it. So Mrs. Kirby went for a walk, wearing the hearing aid. After about half an hour, she returned with tears in her eyes—she hadn't heard birds sing in years.

Well, it wasn't long before the Smiths had the privilege of leading Mrs. Kirby to Jesus. And it wasn't much later that Mrs. Kirby died. Dr. Bob preached at her funeral. "One day I'm going to die and go home to heaven," Dr. Bob observed, "and when I get there I think Mrs. Kirby will be there to greet me. I imagine she will say, 'Dr. Bob, remember that wringer roll?'"

The Smiths used their resources—time, energy, money, and talent—in a way that furthered Christ's kingdom and allowed them to experience and share His presence. Living *coram deo*, in the presence of God, we do what He says and experience His presence more clearly and allow others to experience Him also.

We have the joy not only to lead others to Christ, but to nurture them in Him by emphasizing worship, fellowship, obedience, and stewardship. But there is yet another avenue of growth, and it allows sacramental evangelism to come full circle. It will be the subject of our next, and concluding, chapter.

Discussion Questions

1. Getting a new convert started in individual and corporate worship is essential. Why is so? How could you nurture the new believer in this way?

2. Why is it so important to become a part of a thriving Christian community? Where do you experience fellowship with other believers? Do they constitute an inclusive community that welcomes new converts? How can you help the new believer to value what you have found there?

3. What are the advantages of obedience, as outlined in the text? Which particular benefits have you found most helpful? How can you pass these along to anyone you are following up?

4. Everyone has something by way of time, talent, energy, or resources that can benefit the work of Christ. How can you help the new convert identify specific things he or she can offer? How can stewardship lead to the growth of the giver?

5. Not all children develop in the same way. Do not be afraid to interject more into the nurturing process than the things outlined in these follow-up chapters. Trust that God will give you insight relative to the person you are nurturing in Christ—specific things that will help this individual grow and mature. What would you add to the areas described?

*The sacrament of evangelism is an
invitation to join God in His workplace.*

20) REPRODUCING REPRODUCERS

We have covered a lot of ground in this book, and the finish line is now in sight. Let's gather ourselves before the final sprint. Where is all this going? What have we learned? What exactly is the sacrament of evangelism? Before we can answer that last question, it will be helpful to focus on what it isn't.

So what *isn't* it? Well, the sacrament of evangelism is not a trick or a technique. It is not the latest fad promising us health and wealth. The sacrament is not a recipe for spiritual growth or contentment. It is not a series of tasks on a to-do list. It is not even a series of steps that will lead us to more effective Christian service or more conversions. The sacrament of evangelism is none of these things.

It is instead an invitation to join God in His workplace. The sacrament of evangelism, like our salvation, is not something we reach out and grab. It is a gift we gratefully receive. The sacrament of evangelism comes from God, who walks with us. It tells us He is near and ever at work. More than that, it reveals Him to those of us who have eyes to see. Changing the metaphor a bit, the sacrament of evangelism gives us a front row seat to see His gracious work in the world.

"DECLARE HOW MUCH GOD HAS DONE FOR YOU"

This book, we pray, will open your eyes to the presence of God in your life and in the lives of others. In it we have felt the call to share Christ with others. We have tasted the imperative to abide in Him. We have heard the basic facts about our and others' need for Jesus. And we have seen ways to evangelize and disciple our neighbors so that they experience Him, too. One thing yet remains before the finish. We need to pass the baton. For the sacrament of evangelism, if it *is* a race, is meant to be a relay.

Sometimes we think sacramental evangelism is more difficult than it really is.

God has not only given us the great privilege of leading people to Christ and following them up in their new faith, He has also given us the privilege of reproducing reproducers. He not only wants men and women to come to know Him. He wants to deploy them into the world as witnesses of His love and forgiveness, as those who grasp the sacrament of evangelism.

Jesus knew the sacrament well. In Luke 8 He tells the parable of the sower. The seed is the Word of God. The goal is fruit. Jesus clearly is speaking about evangelism. He follows with an analogy about a lamp. Once a lamp is lit we do not put it under a basket; we let it shine brightly that it might illuminate others. Then the narrative tells of Jesus calming a storm. What's the connection?

In the next scene, Jesus comes ashore in the country of the Gerasenes. There He meets a man with a storm raging in his soul; the man is afflicted by demons. Jesus casts out the invaders and calms the storm in the man's heart. When it is time for Jesus to leave, this grateful man, now in his right mind, asks that he might travel with Jesus.

Jesus simply replies, "Return to your home, and declare how much God has done for you."[1] The man is to go forth and share his testimony about Christ. Proving faithful to his call, the man tells everyone in the city. (In fact, Mark 5:20 says the man proclaimed his story throughout the Decapolis, a region of ten cities.) In this incident Jesus deploys the new convert into the world to tell others. In other words, Jesus seeks to reproduce reproducers. Sacramental evangelists are called to do the same.

HOSPITABLE, NOT PUSHY

Sometimes we think sacramental evangelism is more difficult than it really is. We can begin with a bit of kindness and ask the Lord to direct the conversation, as in the following case.

Once, after Jerry finished preaching in a Sunday morning worship service, he noticed an unfamiliar face in the front pew. Jerry stepped down from the platform and held out his hand: "My name is Jerry," he said. "What's yours?"

"Robert," the young man replied. More questions and answers followed. Jerry wasn't being pushy, but hospitable, and was prepared to go as deep as the visitor would permit.

Jerry asked the young man if he were new to the church, and he said he was. Jerry asked what had brought him to the service. It was a crisis from earlier that week. Robert was a student from the local university. He had gone to church hoping to find some comfort.

"What did you think of the service?" Jerry asked. Robert replied that he had understood most of it but still had a few questions. Jerry answered them the best he could and then asked, "Has anyone ever briefly explained the central message of the Bible to you?" When Robert said, "No," Jerry asked for permission to try, and the young man agreed.

After Jerry explained the gospel, he asked Robert if he would like to trust in Jesus Christ to forgive his sins and invite him to be Lord of his life. Robert, sensing God's presence, replied that he would. The two men prayed together as Robert gave his life to Christ.

Then Jerry told Robert that the Bible's metaphor about beginning a life with Christ is being born again. Jerry pointed out that birth anticipates growth to follow and asked Robert if he would be willing to meet weekly to study the Bible together so they could learn to grow in Christ together. Robert agreed to the meetings.

Over the weeks that followed, they started by looking at what the Bible says about assurance of salvation. Jesus said if we believe in Him, we can be confident that we have eternal life[2] and that this life involves an ever-deepening relationship with Him.[3] They continued by discussing how Jesus is the object of all of our deepest longings.[4]

Jerry's goal in those first couple of weeks was to encourage Robert to fall in love with the God who loved him so deeply, and this in fact began to happen. Over the several weeks, they talked about the importance of regular Bible study so Robert could learn more about God's love and grace. In time he was reading his Bible and praying consistently. Robert was beginning to grow.

As the weeks passed, Robert and Jerry studied the importance of worshiping God and experiencing fellowship in a community where we can be encouraged and nurtured in the faith.[5] They discussed the importance of stewardship of our time, energy, money, and talent.[6] Robert was like a young child awakening to his new world, full of eager questions.

Though the student didn't trust Christ for salvation, he did listen.

The men talked about the importance of obedience and following Christ, even in the difficult circumstances that were sure to come. Robert's eagerness to grow encouraged Jerry's faith. The sacramental presence of Christ was evident in the life change occurring right before Jerry's eyes.

"NERVOUS, BUT EAGER"

The day came when Jerry felt it was time to take Robert out to share his faith in Christ. Jerry wanted to reproduce a reproducer. So they got in the car and drove to the campus where Robert was a student. Here was the plan:

- Jerry would initiate a conversation with someone and attempt to explain the gospel.

- The next time, Jerry would initiate the conversation and ask Robert to share how he came to Christ, then Jerry would take it from there.
- Then with the next person Robert would initiate the conversation and Jerry would back him up.

Robert was nervous but eager. They prayed and went on their way. The campus was large and the weather was perfect. Students were relaxing on the lawn. Some were reading under the warm sun. Others were playing Frisbee. Some were gathered in small groups.

They went up to one young man who was reading and Jerry asked if they could talk about Jesus. Surprised at first, the student kindly let Jerry and Robert visit with him. After Jerry asked some initial questions, the student allowed him to present the gospel. Though the student didn't trust Christ for salvation, he did listen, even asking a few questions of his own. The conversation was easy enough. Jerry and Robert thanked the young man and went on their way.

After some rejections, eventually they came upon two young men. Jerry started the conversation and then asked Robert to share how he came to Christ. Robert articulately described his newfound faith, discovering that this wasn't all that difficult. Neither man responded to the gospel, but the conversation was pleasant.

Finally, it was Robert's turn to initiate. After a refusal or two, Robert was able to go through the entire plan of salvation (which received a polite refusal). No one trusted in Christ that day, but Robert was energized by the outing and told Jerry that some of his friends might also be interested in hearing about Jesus.

STICKING WITH IT

The next week, a day or two before their usual meeting day, Robert told Jerry on the phone that he had reached a sticking place with a friend, Paul, in sharing the gospel. Robert wondered whether he might drive Paul over so that Jerry could answer some of Paul's questions. Twenty minutes later, the three men were sitting in Jerry's office. After exchanging some pleasantries, Jerry asked Paul if he understood what Robert had been sharing with him. Paul said a couple of things were still bothering him. They talked through these issues, and then Jerry, sensing God's sacramental presence, asked Paul if he would like to trust Christ. Paul said yes. Robert was grinning from ear to ear.

He had received a front row seat to watch the God of the universe show up in the sacrament of evangelism. One waits for you as well.

Jerry asked Paul if Robert could pray with him to trust Christ, knowing this would be particularly encouraging to Robert. The two of them prayed together, and Paul became another follower of Christ. Robert began meeting with Paul and going over the same follow-up material that he and Jerry were going over. Robert and Jerry continued to meet, sometimes with Paul joining them. Soon, Robert and Paul were sharing the gospel, and some of their friends came to Christ as well.

THE FRONT ROW SEAT

It wasn't long before Robert told Jerry he was planning to transfer to a college closer to his home so that he could share Christ with family and friends. Several years later, when Jerry was teaching at Wheaton College, Biola University invited him to deliver some lectures and mingle with Talbot Graduate School of Theology students. One morning, as he got out of the rental car at Mimi's restaurant in southern California to meet with them, Jerry was surprised to see Robert getting out of a car one parking place over.

"Robert, what brings you to this neck of the woods?" Jerry cried out. It turned out that Robert was a student at the graduate school. Having seen people in his world come to Jesus, Robert had felt God's call to professional ministry.

After breakfast, they made their way to the campus, where Jerry was to give his first lecture. Outside the auditorium, a young man ran up to Robert, calling out his name, and they greeted each other with joy. Jerry asked the young man, whose name was Michael, how he knew Robert. Michael replied, "Robert is the guy who led me to Jesus!" Jerry's eyes welled up with tears. Moved by the experience, Jerry knew he had received a front row seat to watch the God of the universe show up in the sacrament of evangelism. One waits for you as well.

Jesus offers all of us a front row seat. If we want to see Him at work, we needn't do some esoteric work, some elaborate prayer, or some difficult pilgrimage. We simply need to get to know Him in His workplace, where He is already actively sharing His grace.

Earlier we asked what the sacrament of evangelism is. Now we must ask: Who is it for? The sacrament of evangelism is for every Christian. More than that, it is for you. May the Lord Jesus walk with you as you practice it.

Discussion Questions

I. Helping others discover God's love and forgiveness is important, but why is it vital to take the next step and attempt to reproduce a reproducer?

2. How can you encourage the new believer to take responsibility before Christ for family, friends, and acquaintances in his or her sphere of influence? Why not help the new believer to pray for family, friends, and acquaintances? Would you pray for those he or she includes on the prayer list?

3. What would prevent you from taking a new convert with you to share Christ with someone on his or her list, or someone on your prayer list? Would you remember to always pray with your new ministry partner before sharing the gospel with others?

4. Why is it important for you to model initiating a conversation first before asking the new disciple in Christ to share? How can you bring the young, growing Christian into the gospel presentation while you are witnessing? What should you do while the new disciple attempts to initiate a conversation in order to share the gospel?

5. How can you help the person you are following up begin to follow up those he or she leads to Christ?

NOTES

CHAPTER 1: MISSING OUT

1. Matthew 25:21.
2. Luke 10:38–42.
3. http://campusministry.nd.edu/sacraments.
4. Genesis 28:16b.
5. Westminster Shorter Catechism, http://www.reformed.org/documents/WSC.html.
6. Psalm 19:1.
7. See Romans 1:20.

CHAPTER 2: GETTING STARTED

1. G. K. Chesterton, *What's Wrong with the World?* (Lawrence, Kan., Digireads, a subsidiary of Neeland Media: 2009), 77.
2. Isaiah 55:9
3. Matthew 24:9.
4. 2 Timothy 3:12.
5. Acts 28:20b.

CHAPTER 3: PRAYER

1. Acts 8:26–40.
2. Acts 8:5.
3. Matthew 9:35–38.
4. See Acts 17:26–27.
5. In fact, the Scriptures say without equivocation, in 2 Corinthians 5:18–20, that we are Christ's ambassadors to the world where we live; and that God has given us the ministry of reconciliation to that world, that we might tell people that God was in Christ reconciling the world to Himself.

CHAPTER 4: TARGET PRACTICE

1. Terry Eagleton, *After Theory* (New York: Basic Books, 2003), 137.
2. 1 Corinthians 15:17–19.

3. Ralph Waldo Emerson, The Divinity School Address, "The Second Defect: Revelation Has Ended," http://www.harvardsquarelibrary.org/emerson_hds/The-Second-Defect-Revelation-has-Ended.php.

4. John 1:14a.

5. John Calvin, *The Institutes of the Christian Religion: In Two Volumes*, ed. John T. McNeill, trans. Ford Lewis Battles, vol. 1, book 1, chapter 1, section 1. Library of Christian Classics (Philadelphia: Westminster Press, 1960), 35.

6. *Hamlet*, act 2, scene 2.

7. 2 Samuel 22:29–36.

8. William Finnemore, *The Story of a Hundred Years: 1823–1923* (Oxford: Oxford University Press, 1923), 14, cited at http://www.wmcarey.edu/carey/expect/expect.htm.

9. 2 Chronicles 16:9a NASB.

10. According to researcher D. Michael Lindsey, the proportion of evangelicals among American adults has remained basically the same over the last 30 years, at about a quarter to a third. (See "American Evangelicalism: New Leaders, New Faces, New Issues," Pew Forum on Religion and Public Life, http://pewresearch.org/pubs/883/american-evangelicalism.)

11. Judges 17:6; 21:25.

CHAPTER 5: THE GREAT COMMISSION

1. Matthew 28:18–20.

2. Luke 24:46b–49a.

3. Acts 1:6–8.

4. Esther 4:14.

5. George MacDonald, *Unspoken Sermons*, Second Series, "The Way," http://www.pdfbooks.co.za/library/GEORGE_MACDONALD/GEORGE-UNSPOKEN_SERMONS.pdf, 91.

6. John 3:21.

7. Romans 1:18 NIV.

8. Dietrich Bonhoeffer, *The Cost of Discipleship* (New York: Macmillan, 1937, 1963), 69.

9. See Matthew 14:22–33.

10. 2 Corinthians 6:1, 2b–10.

11. See Elisabeth Elliot, *Through Gates of Splendor* (Peabody, Mass.: Hendrikson, 2010), 160.

12. 2 Corinthians 5:19.

13. Rodney Stark, *The Victory of Reason: How Christianity Led to Freedom,*

Capitalism, and Western Success (New York: Random House, 2005), xi.

14. Matthew 22:37–39.
15. Luke 4:16–21.

CHAPTER 6: DISCOVERING GOD'S LOVE

1. John 15:1–2, 4–5.
2. Luke 6:43–44a.
3. C. S. Lewis, *Mere Christianity* (New York: HarperSanFrancisco, 2001), 125.
4. Galatians 6:1a.
5. Philip Yancey, "Honest Church Marketing," *Christianity Today*, October 22, 2001, http://www.christianitytoday.com/ct/2001/october22/29.112.html.
6. 1 John 4:18.
7. Francis Thompson, *The Hound of Heaven* (New York: Dodd, Mead and Company, 1926), quoted in http://www.gutenberg.org/files/30730/30730-h/30730-h.htm.
8. Jeremiah 2:13.
9. http://www.imdb.com/title/tt0332280/quotes.

CHAPTER 7: RESPONDING TO HIS LOVE

1. Matthew 24:12b.
2. Mark 12:28–34.
3. Habakkuk 3:17–18.
4. Luke 22:31–34, 54–62.
5. Mark 16:7.
6. Dorothy Sayers, "The Triumph of Easter" *Creed or Chaos?* (New York: Harcourt, Brace, 1949), new ed.: (Manchester, N.H.: Sophia Institute Press, 1974), 17.
7. John 21:15–19.

CHAPTER 8: THE SPIRIT: GOD'S ABIDING AND EMPOWERING PRESENCE

1. John 14:12.
2. See Philippians 2:5–8 for Paul's summary of Christ's self-emptying ministry, a ministry we are to emulate.
3. John 14:16–21, 23.
4. Again, see Philippians 2:5–8. Jesus obediently humbled Himself to do the

Father's will.

5. Acts 1:8.
6. Mark 1:8.
7. 1 Corinthians 12:13 NIV.
8. Ephesians 4:22–24.
9. Ephesians 5:15–16.
10. Ephesians 5:17b–18.
11. 1 John 1:9.
12. 1 John 5:14–15.
13. These lists are not exhaustive.
14. Exodus 31:1–6.
15. Judges 14:6, 19; 15:14.
16. Galatians 5:22–23a.
17. 2 Corinthians 2:14.

CHAPTER 9: CHARACTER: HABITS OF THE HEART

1. Acts 5:27–32, 40–42.
2. John 21:18–19.
3. 2 Peter 1:5b–11.
4. See Peter Kreeft, "Justice, Wisdom, Courage, and Moderation: The Four Cardinal Virtues," Chapter 4 in *Back to Virtue* (San Francisco: Ignatius Press, 1986), 59–70, quoted by Peter Kreeft, "Justice, Wisdom, Courage, and Moderation: The Four Cardinal Virtues," Catholic Education Resource Center, http://www.catholiceducation.org/articles/religion/re0017.html.
5. Quoted in *Plato's Concept of Justice: An Analysis*, by D. R. Bhandari, http://www.bu.edu/wcp/Papers/Anci/AnciBhan.htm.
6. Quoted in BrainyQuote, http://www.brainyquote.com/quotes/authors/s/saint_augustine.html.
7. Quoted in BrainyQuote, http://www.brainyquote.com/quotes/authors/s/saint_augustine_3.html.
8. Hebrews 13:8.

CHAPTER 10: MIRRORING THE PRESENCE OF CHRIST IN THE WORLD

1. John 3:30.
2. Exodus 3:14.
3. Exodus 3:11.

4. Exodus 3:12.

5. See Colossians 2:20–3:3.

6. 2 Corinthians 5:17–21.

7. Hans Rookmaaker, as reported by Nigel Goodwin and others at L'Abri in Huemoz, Switzerland, as referenced in Dick Staub, *The Culturally Savvy Christian: A Manifesto for Deepening Faith and Enriching Popular Culture in an Age of Christianity-Lite* (San Francisco: Jossey-Bass, 2007), xv.

CHAPTER 11: POINTS OF CONNECTION

1. Stan Guthrie, "The Changing Face of Apologetics," *Christianity Today*, June 2009, http://www.christianitytoday.com/ct/2009/june/22.58.html.

2. John 4:4–41.

3. Friedrich von Hugel, *Letters from Friedrich Von Hugel to a Niece*, ed. with an introduction by Gwendolen Greene (London & Toronto: J. M. Dent & Sons Ltd., 1932), x.

4. Miller McPherson, Lynn Smith-Lovin, and Matthew E. Brashears, "Social Isolation in America," *American Sociological Review* 71 (2006): 353–75.

5. See Philippians 2:15 NIV.

6. Dale Carnegie, *How to Win Friends and Influence People* (New York: Simon & Schuster, 2009), 99–103.

7. See, for example, 1 Corinthians 1:26–31.

8. See Matthew 25:14–30.

9. See Stan Guthrie, *All That Jesus Asks: How His Questions Can Teach and Transform Us* (Grand Rapids: Baker, 2010).

10. John 3:1–8.

11. Merriam-Webster OnLine, "analogy," http://www.merriam-webster.com/dictionary/analogy.

12. See John 5.

13. Von Hugel, *Letters*, x.

14. Anne Lamott, *Traveling Mercies: Some Thoughts on Faith* (New York: Anchor Books, 1999), 134.

15. Albert Schweitzer, *The Philosophy of Civilization: The Decay and the Restoration of Civilization*, vol. 1 (London: A & C Black, Ltd., 1947), 2.

CHAPTER 12: LONGING: *PILGRIM*

1. Evelyn Underhill, *Mysticism: A Study in Nature and Development of Spiritual Consciousness*, Christian Classics Ethereal Library, http://www.ccel.org/ccel/underhill/mysticism.txt.

2. J. R. R. Tolkien, *The Hobbit* (Boston: Houghton Mifflin, 1966), 11.

3. 1 Peter 1:1 NIV.

4. Hebrews 11:8–16.

5. G. K. Chesterton, "The House of Christmas," quoted in "The Journey with Jesus: Poems and Prayers," selected by Dan Clendenin, http://www.jour neywithjesus.net/PoemsAndPrayers/GK_Chesterton_House_of_Christ mas.shtml.

6. Environmentally attuned Christians, of course, do not believe the earth is our only home but see creation care as a matter of stewardship.

7. Saint Augustine, *The Confessions*, trans. by Maria Boulding, O.S.B. (New York: New City Press, 1997), 14.

8. Sheldon Vanauken, *A Severe Mercy* (San Francisco: Harper & Row, 1977), 93.

9. J. I. Packer and Jerry Root, "Mind in Motion: He tasted many philosophies, but he was always stuck on reality," *Christian History & Biography* issue 88 (Fall 2005):16.

CHAPTER 13: LONGING: *LOVER*

1. Dante Alighieri, *Vita Nuova*, trans. with an introduction by Mark Musa (Oxford: Oxford University Press, 1992, XXIV), 52.

2. S. Morris Guthrie, *A Short Report on Guthrie Genealogy as It's Known Today*, "The Story of Henry Guthrie," unpublished report, August 9, 2005.

3. Noted in, among many others, Bruce L. Edwards, *C. S. Lewis: Life, Works, and Legacy* (Westport, Conn.: Greenwood Publishing, 2007), 35.

4. Ecclesiastes 1:14.

5. Mark 8:36.

6. Matthew 7:24–27.

CHAPTER 14: LONGING: *ASCETIC/SAINT*

1. Romans 3:23.

2. Plato, *Apology*, trans. by Benjamin Jowett *Great Books of the Western World*, Robert Maynard Hutchins editor in chief (Chicago: Encyclopedia Britan- nica, 1952), 210.

3. *The Cloud of Unknowing and Other Works*, trans. into Modern English with an introduction by Clifton Wolters (London: Penguin Books, 1978), 78.

4. Rob Moll, "Saved by an Atheist," *Christianity Today*, August 2010, 40.

5. Matthew 7:21.

6. Matthew 13:24–30, 36–43.

CHAPTER 15: OTHER LONGINGS

1. See C. S. Lewis, "Learning in War-Time: A sermon preached in the Church of St. Mary the Virgin, Oxford, autumn, 1939," http://www.calvin.edu/~pribeiro/DCM-Lewis-2009/Lewis/learning%20in%20wartime.doc.
2. Viktor E. Frankl, *Man's Search for Meaning* (New York: Washington Square Press, 1985), 88.
3. Thomas Traherne, *Centuries of Meditations*, I. 23, quoted in Spirit of Prayer, http://www.spiritofprayer.com/01century.php.
4. Matthew 6:24.
5. David Taylor, "A Holy Longing: Beauty is the hard-to-define essence that draws people to the gospel," *Christianity Today*, October 2008, http://www.christianitytoday.com/ct/2008/october/17.39.html.
6. See Acts 8–9:18.

CHAPTER 16: WHO WE ARE

1. Jean Twenge, *Generation Me: Why Today's Young Americans Are More Confident, Assertive, Entitled—and More Miserable than Ever Before* (New York: Free Press, 2007), 36.
2. Romans 1:28–32.
3. Russell Kirk, *The Conservative Mind: From Burke to Eliot*, seventh rev. ed. (Washington, D.C.: Regnery Gateway, 1953, 2001), 27.
4. Genesis 1:26–27.
5. Genesis 3.
6. John Calvin, *Institutes of the Christian Religion. Selections from Institutes of the Christian Religion*, trans. by Henry Beveridge ed in chief, Mortimer J. Adler, vol. 20 (Chicago: Encyclopedia Britannica, 1994), bk. I, ch. XIV, sec. 3, 63.
7. Ibid., bk. I, ch. XV, sec. 4. 75–76.
8. Quoted in Andrew Finstuen, *Original Sin and Everyday Protestants: The Theology of Reinhold Niebuhr, Billy Graham, and Paul Tillich in an Age of Anxiety* (Chapel Hill, N.C.: University of North Carolina Press, 2009), 69.
9. Ephesians 2:1.
10. C. H. Spurgeon, "A Defense of Calvinism," Spurgeon Archive, http://www.spurgeon.org/calvinis.htm.
11. See, for example, 2 Corinthians 5:15.
12. John 10:27.
13. Matthew 5:45.
14. Acts 14:17.
15. Romans 2:4.

16. Romans 1:18.

17. Frederick Buechner, *Telling the Truth: The Gospel as Comedy, Tragedy and Fairy Tale* (New York: HarperOne, 1977), 7.

18. C. S. Lewis, "Christian Apologetics," *God in the Dock: Essays on Theology and Ethics*, ed. Walter Hooper (Grand Rapids: Eerdmans, 1970), 96.

CHAPTER 17: COMMUNICATION

1. Quoted in Jerry Root and Claudia Root, *Friendship Evangelism* (Wheaton: Harold Shaw, 1990), 17.

2. Tried-and-true methods such as Roman Road and the Four Spiritual Laws can be readily found online.

3. 1 John 4:8.

4. John 3:16.

5. Genesis 3:1–13.

6. Ephesians 2:1.

7. Romans 5:1–10.

8. Romans 1:16.

9. Romans 6:22–23.

10. C. S. Lewis, *Surprised by Joy: The Shape of My Early Life* (Ft. Washington, Penn.: Harvest Books, 2002).

11. "Did You Know? Interesting and unusual facts about C. S. Lewis," *Christian History & Biography* issue 88 (fall 2005): 2.

12. Joshua 24:15.

13. http://www.campuscrusade.com/fourlawseng.htm.

14. http://www.navigators.org/resources/shared/tools/bridge.pdf.

15. D. James Kennedy, *Evangelism Explosion*, 4th ed. (Wheaton: Tyndale, 1996).

16. D. James Kennedy, *Evangelism Explosion*, third ed. (Wheaton: Tyndale, 1983), 17–18.

17. See Thomas A. Howard's introduction to Malcolm Muggeridge, *A Twentieth Century Testimony* (Nashville: Thomas Nelson, 1978).

CHAPTER 18: FOLLOW-UP #1: JESUS, PRAYER, AND BIBLE STUDY

1. John 6:47 and 1 John 5:11–12 say clearly that faith in Christ for the forgiveness of sins assures us of eternal life. Eternal life is endless. If it could be lost after it has been given, then it is not truly eternal.

2. John 17:3.

3. Nicene Creed, see http://www.creeds.net/ancient/nicene.htm.

4. See Luke 5:1–11.
5. See John 7:32–52.
6. See Luke 4:20–30.
7. Matthew 7:28b–29.
8. See Matthew 14:13–21.
9. See Matthew 8:23–27.
10. Mark 2:1–12.
11. John 14:6b.
12. Aristotle, quoted by "QuoteDB," http://www.quotedb.com/quotes/917.
13. John 10:24–33.
14. See John 6.
15. See Matthew 13:44–46.
16. Hebrews 12:2a.
17. George MacDonald, quoted in Thomas Guthrie, William Garden Blaikie, Benjamin Waugh, *The Sunday Magazine*, vol. 13 (London: Ibister and Company, 1883), 574.
18. 2 Timothy 3:14–17.
19. Psalm 19:1.
20. Romans 1:20a.
21. See John 3:3–7.
22. 1 Peter 2:2.
23. 1 Corinthians 9:24–25.

CHAPTER 19: FOLLOW-UP #2: WORSHIP, FELLOWSHIP, OBEDIENCE, AND STEWARDSHIP

1. Hebrews 10:24–25.
2. See the discussion about the nature of justice in chapter 9.
3. See Exodus 20:11.
4. 1 Corinthians 10:31.
5. 1 Corinthians 12:12–13.
6. Lewis B. Smedes, "CT Classic: Forgiveness—The Power to Change the Past," *Christianity Today*, January 7, 1983. Quote available at http://www.ctlibrary.com/ct/2002/decemberweb-only/12-16-55.0.html; electronic access to full article requires paid membership.
7. Jean Jacques Rousseau, *The Social Contract or Principles of Political Right*, bk. 1, The Great Books of the Western World, vol. 38 (Chicago: Encyclopedia Britannica, 1952), 387.

CHAPTER 20: REPRODUCING REPRODUCERS

1. Luke 8:39a.
2. John 10:28.
3. 2 Peter 1:3–9.
4. See chapters 12–15.
5. See chapter 18.
6. See chapter 19.

SUBJECT INDEX

Abortion, 193–94
Abraham, 153–54
Acts, 59, 60, 111
Adam and Eve, 10, 207
Aeneas, 150
Aeneid, The, 151
Agape (charity), 92, 215
All-American, 28, 30
Alexander the Great, 188
Alverez, Jesus, 98–99
Amadeus, 85
American Sociological Review, 139
Ananias, 195
Anthropology (biblical), 204
Ascetic/Saint, 173–85
Asking questions, 141–44
Aristotle, 116, 231
Ascension, 101
Audience (see Target), 48
Augustine, 80, 116, 118, 119, 155
Authenticity, 27, 192–93
Awkwardness, 23–24, 30, 32

Baptism by the Holy Spirit, 102, 104
Barak, 56

Beamer, Lisa, 187
Beamer, Todd, 187
Beatrice, 161–63, 170
Beauty, 194–95
Beeson Divinity School, 10
Bethel College and Seminary, 248
Bible, 10, 19, 31, 47, 48, 65, 73, 74, 83, 85, 98, 106, 116, 140, 167, 168, 202, 246, 256
Bible study, 233, 235–38, 239, 242
Bilbo Baggins, 151
Billy Graham Center at Wheaton College, 222
Biola University, 260
Bitterness, 145
Black Madonna, 150
Bodleian Library at Oxford University, 118
Body of Christ, 102
Bonhoeffer, Dietrich, 62
Brother Lawrence, 14
Brashears, Matthew E., 139
Buechner, Frederick, 209, 210
Bullet, 47–48, 50, 52, 57
Burning bush, 125

California, 97
Calvin, John, 51, 206
Campus Crusade for Christ,
    103, 222
Capernaum, 229
Caribou, 143
Carey, William, 54
Carnegie, Dale, 139
Cassavetes, Nick, 77
Catholics, 15, 149
Charity, 118
Chesterton, G. K., 10, 22, 23,
    154, 157, 213
Chicago, 194, 222
Chicago Cubs, 149
Christians, 151
Christmas, 18, 155
Christology, 204
Christ's Ambassadors, 39, 127
Christ Church College,
    Oxford University, 175
Church, 15, 19, 64, 66, 72,
    112, 116, 127–128, 174,
    245, 246
Claiborne, Shane, 66
Cloud of Unknowing, The,
    179–80, 184
Cobb County Georgia, 164
Confession, 103, 107
Courage, 35, 113, 114–115,
    119, 120
Covington, Georgia, 164
Cross (of Christ), 79, 216,
    217, 220

Cross-cultural missionaries, 67
Culture of evangelism, 54
Current events, 143, 146
Czestochowa, Poland, 150

Daniel, 16
Dante, 161–63, 170
David, 16, 53
Day, Dick, 29–30
Death, 143, 188
Decapolis, 255
Denmark, 52
Depravity, 203, 205, 206, 207
Desert Fathers, 174
Diagnostic questions, 86–94
Dialectic of Desire, The,
    165–67
Dickens, Charles, 152
Disciples, 23, 38, 64, 71, 100,
    101, 137, 228–29, 232–33
Discipleship, 14, 242
Discipline, 247
Disobedience, 62
Divine Comedy, The, 161–62
Dorsett, Lyle, 10

Eagleton, Terry, 47
East Los Angeles, 99
Ecclesiastes, 166–67
Egypt, 16, 126
El Centro, California, 97–98
Eldorado, 149
Elliot, Jim, 63
Emerson, Ralph Waldo, 49–50

England, 179
Ephesus, 102
Episteme (Skill; root word for
  epistemology), 118

Eros, 215
Esther, 61
Ethiopian eunuch, 37
Eternal life, 227, 256
Europe, 65, 178
Evangelicals, 15, 64, 74
Evangelism, 14, 16, 23, 26,
  28, 30, 32, 35, 36, 37, 41,
  43, 52, 53, 54, 56, 57, 59,
  62, 64, 66, 70, 79, 85, 90,
  91, 101, 110, 112, 113,
  115, 124, 174, 183, 203,
  209, 212, 213–14, 220,
  247, 249. 252, 253, 254,
  255, 259, 260
Evangelism Explosion, 222
Evangelists, 38, 49, 52, 55,
  110, 112, 122, 127, 142,
  155, 156, 163, 166, 170,
  175, 186, 190, 191, 196,
  201, 213, 221, 222, 226,
  227, 248
Evil, 203
Exegete, 47

Faith, 214, 257, 258
False infinite, 191
Fear, 62, 75–76
Fellowship, 240, 244–46, 249,

250, 257
Figure of Beatrice, The, 161

Filling of the Holy Spirit, 102,
  104
Florence, Italy 161
Football, 28, 83
Forgiveness, 205, 216, 230,
  246, 254, 256, 261
Frankl, Viktor, 189
Frisbee, 258
Fruit of the Spirit, 105

Gandalf, 151
Garner, James, 77–79
Gaza, 37
Generation Me, 201
Gerasene demoniac, 255
Gideon, 56
Ginosko (experiential
  knowledge), 118
God, 9, 10, 14–15, 16, 17, 18,
  19, 20, 25, 26, 28, 30, 32,
  36, 37, 38, 39, 41, 42, 43,
  48, 49, 51, 52, 53, 54, 56,
  60, 61, 62, 63, 65, 66, 67,
  71, 75, 76, 79, 80, 85, 86,
  87, 88, 89, 90, 91, 93, 98,
  102, 103, 104, 107, 108,
  111, 112, 116, 122, 123,
  124, 126, 127, 128, 129,
  130, 137, 139, 139, 143,
  144, 145, 154, 156, 157,
  158, 163, 164, 165, 166,

167, 168, 169, 170, 171,
172, 174, 175, 176, 177,
178, 182, 183, 184, 189,
190, 191, 192, 194, 195,
196, 197, 203, 204, 205,
206, 207, 208, 207, 209,
210, 214, 215, 216, 217,
218, 219, 220, 221, 222,
227, 228, 230, 231–32,
233, 234, 239, 240, 241,
242, 244, 245, 246, 247,
249, 250, 252, 253, 256,
261
Goliath, 16
Good news, 17, 30, 36, 37,
    65, 200, 203, 209, 210
Good, the True, and the
    Beautiful, The 192–95
Gospel, 20, 21, 23, 32, 33, 35,
    37, 38, 43, 48, 49, 50, 52,
    57, 64, 65, 94, 127, 135,
    140, 196, 200, 210, 214,
    215, 217, 224, 261
Gospel According to Peanuts,
    The, 84
Gospel *words* and gospel
    works (see kingdom *words*
    and kingdom *works*),
    68, 128
Grace, 207, 209, 210
Graham, Billy, 66, 222–23
Great Commandment, 10,
    66, 68
Great Commission, 10, 58,

59, 60, 64, 65, 66, 67, 68
Great Expectations, 152
Gun, 51, 52, 57
Guthrie, Christine, 83–8
Guthrie, Henry, 164
Guthrie, Stan, 9, 10, 31, 35,
    83–85, 135, 149, 164,
    180–81, 218–220, 222–23,
    241–42, 246

Habits, 113–119
Habakkuk, 89–90
Hamlet, 52
Harry Potter, 175
Harvard Divinity School, 49
Harvest, 38, 43
Havard, Robert E., 218
Heaven, 153, 227
Hegel, Georg Wilhelm
    Friedrich, 165
Hierarchy, 168
High Table, 175–78
Hindu, 35
Hobbit, The, 151
Hogwarts, 175
Holiness, 102
Holy Spirit, 43, 59, 63, 66, 96,
    99, 100, 101, 102, 103,
    104, 106, 107, 108, 111,
    112, 155, 223, 235, 242
Homesick at home, 154–55,
    157
Homer, 150
Honesty, 52, 118, 169, 182,

185, 232, 243
Hound of Heaven, The, 76
How to Win Friends and Influence People, 139
Human nature 202–09
Humility, 52, 124, 125, 169, 179–80, 185, 232, 243
Huntington Park, California, 106
Hypocrites, 27, 182–83
Hypocrisy, 181–83

Ignorance, 140
Image of God, 10, 144, 145, 206, 222
India, 35
Injustice, 117
Institutes of the Christian Religion, 264
InterVarsity Christian Fellowship, 83
Israel, 54, 55, 60, 126

Jacob, 16, 136
Jalisco, Mexico, 97–100
Jeremiah, 16
Jericho, 55
Jerusalem, 60, 101
Jesus Christ, 9, 13, 14, 16, 17, 20, 23, 24, 25, 26, 28, 29, 30, 32, 33, 36, 38, 39, 41, 42, 43, 44, 48, 49, 51, 52, 54, 57, 59, 60, 61, 62, 64, 66, 67, 72, 73, 74, 79, 85,

86, 87, 88, 90, 91, 92, 93, 94, 98, 100, 101, 102, 103, 106, 107, 111, 112, 113, 114, 115, 119, 120, 124, 127, 128, 129, 131, 135, 136, 137, 140, 141, 142, 145, 160, 164, 167, 169, 176, 179, 181, 182, 183, 184, 186, 195, 196, 197, 206, 208, 209, 214, 216, 217, 218, 219, 220, 221, 222, 223, 224, 226, 227–33, 239, 242, 244, 245, 246, 247, 249, 250, 255, 256, 257, 258, 259, 261
Job, 167
John the Baptist, 125
Jordan River, 55
Joseph (son of Jacob), 136
Joshua, 55
Judea, 101
Just As I Am, 42
Justice, 64, 114, 116–118, 119, 120

Keillor, Garrison, 201
Kingdom words and Kingdom works (see gospel words and gospel works), 67
Kirk, Russell, 203
Knowledge, 113
Krakow, Poland, 149–50

Laborers, 38

Lake Wobegon, 201
Lamott, Anne, 145
Latin America, 97
"Learning in War–Time," 188
Lewis, C. S., 10, 72, 74, 80,
    155, 156, 161, 164–65,
    184, 188, 209, 218, 233
Liberal arts, 140–41
Lindsey, D. Michael, 264
Little Green Valley YMCA
    Camp, 106
Liturgical, 15
Los Angeles, 106
Los Estados Unidos, 98
Love, 215
Lover longing, 161–71
Luke 59, 60, 111
Lutreo (worship through
    service), 243
Lydia, 9
Lyons, Minerva, 164

MacDonald, George, 10,
    61–62, 233–34
Man's Search for Meaning, 189
Marriage, 163–64
Martha, 13–14
Mary (mother of Jesus),
    13–14
Mary Magdalene, 91–92
Matthew, 229
Marx, Karl, 150
McPherson, Miller, 139
Meaning, 189–90

Mecca, 150
Mere Christianity, 73
Metaphor, 49, 124, 256
Methodist, 84
Mexicali, Mexico, 97
Midian Wilderness, 125
Miracles, 100
Moll, Rob, 182
Moody, D. L., 213
Mordecai, 61
Moses, 16, 125–126, 130
Mother Teresa, 66
Muggeridge, Malcolm, 223
Music, 144
Muslims, 150

Navigators, The, 222
Nazareth, 66
Nebuchadnezzar II, 188
New Atheism, 72
New York, 187
New Testament, 60, 92, 243
Nicodemus, 141–42, 236
Northern lights, 18
Notebook, The, 77–79

Obedience, 61–62, 63, 67,
    124, 125, 245, 246–47,
    249, 250
Odysseus, 150
The Odyssey, 150
Oida (head knowledge), 118
Ordo amoris (ordered love),
    168

Original sin, 207
Oxford University, 14, 175

Packer, J. I., 156
Paul, 9, 31, 39, 47, 59, 62,
    74, 102, 103, 105, 206,
    235–36, 237, 244
Pennsylvania, 187
Pentecost, 16
Peter, 16, 62, 91–93, 111, 112,
    113, 116, 117, 118, 153,
    233
Pew pastors, 128
Pharaoh, 126
Pharisees, 228
Philia (friendship), 92, 215
Philip, 37
Philippi, 9
Pilgrim longing, 149–58
Pilgrim's Regress, The, 156
Plato, 116, 192
Points of connection, 136 ff.
    138, 139
Polio, 205
Polonius, 52–53
Ponte Vecchio, The, 161
Pool of Bethesda, 142
Postmodern, 135
Prayer, 35, 37, 38, 40, 43,
    233–34, 239, 242
Pretense, 51
Pride, 73–74, 124
Proclamation, 65
Promised Land, 55

Proskuneo (see Worship), 243
Protestants, 15
Proverbs, 167
Psalms, 167

Rationalization, 51
RCA Dome, Indianapolis,
    Indiana, 222
Republic, The, 116
Red Sea, 16
Religion, 124–125
Repentance, 216
Rhetoric, 64
Rowlands, Gena, 77
Rome, 31, 150
Romantics, 178
Rookmaaker, Hans, 129
Root, Alicia, 41
Root, Jeremy, 152–53
Root, Jerry, 9, 10, 28–30,
    39–42, 47, 77, 86–87, 97,
    105–106, 115–116, 123,
    140, 152–53, 156, 161–62,
    168–70, 173–74, 175–78,
    187, 192–94, 205, 221,
    238, 255–61
Rousseau, Jean–Jacques, 203,
    247

Sacrament, 9, 15, 16, 17, 20,
    21, 23, 37, 39, 41, 42, 43,
    49, 52, 53, 55, 59, 62, 70,
    79, 85, 86, 91, 110, 112,
    113, 122, 124, 127, 142,

155, 156, 163, 166, 170, 174, 175, 181, 182, 183, 186, 190, 191, 196, 201, 203, 209, 213–14, 220, 221, 226, 227, 242, 247, 248, 249, 252, 253, 254, 255, 259, 260
Salk, Jonas, 205

Salvation (see Soteriology), 208
Samaria, 101, 136
San Diego State University, 201
Sanford Universit,y 10
Sarras, 149
Saul (see Paul), 195
Savoir, 111, 113, 119
Sayers, Dorothy, 10, 92, 161
Schweitzer, Albert, 145
Scripture, 18, 47, 51, 54, 67, 73, 91, 100, 102, 192, 201, 208, 217, 227, 243
Sea of Galilee, 229
Seeker, 48
Self-knowledge, 50–52, 57
September 11, 2001 (9–11), 187, 189, 190
Service, 243
Shakespeare, 52
Short, Robert, 84
Sin, 89, 107, 201–02, 203, 204, 205, 206, 207, 216,

217, 220, 230, 232, 245, 256
Smedes, Louis B., 246
Smith, Dr. Bob, 248–49
Smith–Lovin, Lynn, 139
The Social Contract, 247
Social ministry, 65
Socrates, 116
Solidarity, 150, 179
Song of Solomon, The, 167
Soteriology (the doctrine of salvation; see Salvation), 204–05
Sparks, Nicholas, 77
Spiritual breathing, 103
Spiritual gifts, 103–104
Spiritual maturity, 20, 88, 115
Spiritual thirst, 39
Spurgeon, C. H., 208
St. Peter's Basilica, Rome, 149
Starbucks, 143
Stark, Rodney, 65
Stewardship, 247–249, 250, 257
Story, 135
Stott, John, 192–93
Strobel, Lee, 135
Suffering, 189
Surprised by Joy: The Shape of My Early Life, 218

Talbot Graduate School of Theology, 260

Target (see Audience), 48–49,
  50, 52, 57
Taylor, David, 195
Temperance, 114, 115–116,
  119, 120
Temptation, 245
Thanksgiving, 149
Theology, 200, 203, 204
Theology proper (the
  doctrine of God), 204
Thompson, Francis, 76, 80
Time, 155–56
Timothy, 235
Tolkien, J. R. R. ,151
Traherne, Thomas, 191
Trinity (God), 204
"The Triumph of Easter," 92
Troy, 150
Truth, 48, 137, 215, 231
Twenge, Jean, 201

UFOs, 219
Upper Room Discourse, 71
Underhill, Evelyn, 10, 149,
  156, 163, 174–75
United Flight, 93 187
University of Florida Gators,
  83
University of Notre Dame, 15
Unspoken Sermons, 61–62
Ur of the Chaldeans, 153–54

Virgil, 150
Virtue, 113–119
Vita Nuova, 162
Von Hugel, Baron Friedrich,
  138, 144

Western churches, 54
Western culture, 142
Westminster Catechism, 17
Widener Library, Harvard
  College, 118
Williams, Charles, 161
Winchester, 38 Special, 47
Wisdom, 114, 118–119, 120
Wheaton College, 140, 152,
  187, 222, 260
White House, 187
Whittier College, 28, 86
Wordsworth, William, 178–79
Workplace, 19, 21
World Trade Center, 187
World War II, 248
Worship, 242, 243–44, 249,
  257
Wrestling, 238
Wrigley Field, Chicago, 149

Yancey, Philip, 74
YMCA, 106–107

SCRIPTURE INDEX

Genesis
1 — 125
1:26–27 — 206
3 — 206
3:1–13 — 216
28:16 — 16

Exodus
3:11 — 126
3:12 — 126
3:14 — 125
20:11 — 243
31:1–6 — 104

Joshua
24:15 — 221

Judges
2:10 — 55
14:6, 19; 15:14 — 104
17:6; 21:25 — 54

2 Samuel
22:29–36 — 53–54

2 Chronicles
16:9 — 54

Esther
4:14 — 62

Psalms
19:1 — 18, 236

Proverbs
15:22 — 118

Ecclesiastes
1:1–2 — 166
2:25 — 166–67
3:11 — 167
12:13 — 167

Isaiah
55:9 — 27
64:6 — 125

Jeremiah
2:13 — 76

Habakkuk
3:17–18 — 89

Matthew
5:45 — 209
7:21 — 182
7:24–27 — 168
7:28b–29 — 229
8:23–27 — 229
9:35–38 — 38, 50
13:24–30, 36–43 — 182
13:44–46 — 233
14:13–21 — 229

14:22–33 — 62
22:37–39 — 66
24:9 — 31
24:12 — 85
25:21 — 13
25:14–30 — 141
28:18–20 — 10, 59

Mark
1:8 — 102
2:1–2 — 230
5:20 — 255
8:36 — 167
12:29–31 — 10, 86
16:7 — 92

Luke
4:16–21 — 66–67
4:20–30 — 229
5:1–11 — 228
6:43–44 — 73
8 — 254
8:39 — 255
10:38–42 — 14–15
11:13 — 206
24:46–49 — 60

John
1:1 — 50
3:1–8 — 141–42, 236
3:16 — 215
3:21 — 62

3:30	125	5:8	51	**Colossians**		
4:4–41	136–138	6:22–23	216–17	1:24	31	
5	142	7:18	206	2:20–3:3	127	
6	14	12:7–11	104	**2 Timothy**		
6:47	227			3:12	31	
7:32–52	229	**1 Corinthians**		3:14–17	235	
9:1–5	220	1:26–31	140			
10:24–33	231–32	9:24–25	237–38	**Hebrews**		
10:27	209	10:31	244	10:24–25	242–43	
10:28	256	12:12–13	245	11:8–16	153–54	
14:6	231	12:13	102	12:2a	233	
14:12	100	15:17–19	48	13:8	119	
14:16–23	101					
15:1–2, 4–5	71	**2 Corinthians**		**Philemon**		
17:3	227	2:14	105	6	25, 26	
21:18–19	112	5:15	208			
		5:18–21	65, 127,	**1 Peter**		
Acts			218, 263	1:5–11	113	
1:8	101	6:1, 2–10	63	2:2	236	
5:27–32, 40–42	112			2:24	217	
8–9:18	195	**Galatians**				
14:17	209	5:22–23	105	**2 Peter**		
16:14	9	6:1	74	1:1–11	113, 120	
17:26–27	39			1:3–9	256	
28:20	31	**Ephesians**				
		2:1	208, 216	**1 John**		
Romans		4:22–24	102	1:9	103	
1:16	216	5:15–16	102	4:8	215	
1:18	62, 209	5:18	103	4:17	124	
1:20	18, 236			4:18	75	
1:28–32	201–02	**Philippians**		4:20	90	
2:4	209	2:5–8	265	5:11–12	218, 227	
3:23	173			5:14–15	103	
5:1–10	216					

ACKNOWLEDGMENTS

Jerry:

I would like to thank my wife, Claudia, for the sacrifices of time she made while I worked on this manuscript and for her model of witness that has been evident in her life since we first met; and my sister Kathy for the kind offer to use her home in Bodega Bay as an escape where much of this work was written. I have deep heartfelt gratitude to Stan Guthrie, who knows his craft and knows how to both start and finish a project and to do everything necessary in between. I am also grateful to Jean Bilang for editorial advice she gave along the way. My brother, Chester, Robert Seelye, Verl Lindley, Mark Neuenschwander, Dick Day, Chris Claydon, Gary Whisenand, and Pokey Cleek were embodiments of the material of this book and their examples have made an indelible impression on me; my debt to them is great. Furthermore, nearly three decades of collegial conversation about evangelism with Lyle Dorsett have shaped and honed so many of the ideas in this book. I am also grateful to the Mead Men: Lon

Allison, David Henderson, Brian Medaglia, Chris Mitchell, and Rick Richardson for their important critical responses to the text during the various stages of its development; no book can be written without intentional feedback such as they took time to give. My friend Tim Tremblay and his wife, Marcia, have been participants with me in doing personal evangelism, and I am grateful to them as well. Furthermore, I would like to thank my students at both Wheaton College and Biola University who have taken this material and applied it in order to see many come to Christ over the years, demonstrating to me that it has transferability to others. And, lastly, I want to thank Mark Noll for many years of unexpected notes and words of encouragement that made me think I could engage in the work of writing.

Stan:

My thanks, first of all, go to Christine, who has been called into an even more challenging role than before and has handled it, as expected, with her usual grace and toughness. She has enabled me, now more than ever, to pursue worthy projects such as this one. You get little notoriety now, Sweetheart, but I expect to hear the Lord's "Well done, good and faithful servant" for you one day. Thanks also to my parents, Morris and Irene Guthrie, for their continual encouragement. My gratitude also flows to Jerry Root, who has showered me with kindness, fellowship, and encouragement following the unlooked-for renewal of our friendship. Truly, you live the words of this book. Our sincere appreciation also goes to Randall Payleitner of Moody Publishers for believing in this volume and for offering helpful support along the way.

AN ANCHOR FOR THE SOUL

People have honest doubts and questions about God that deserve solid answers. How do we explain the gospel of Jesus Christ in a way we can all understand? Ray Pritchard has updated this bestselling presentation of the gospel in a clear, straightforward way using simple language and clear Scripture references.

An Anchor for the Soul is written with doubters, seekers, and skeptics in mind. It answers questions such as: What is God like? How can I know Him? Who is Jesus and what did He do? What does it mean to be a Christian? Through stories and illustrations, Pastor Pritchard very personally, yet gently, challenges his readers with the Good News of Jesus Christ.

MOODY
PUBLISHERS

moodypublishers.com